# The Motion Picture Goes to War
## The U.S. Government Film Effort during World War I

# Studies in Cinema, No. 37

## Diane M. Kirkpatrick, Series Editor

Professor, History of Art
The University of Michigan

## Other Titles in This Series

# The Motion Picture Goes to War
## The U.S. Government Film Effort during World War I

by
Larry Wayne Ward

UMI RESEARCH PRESS
Ann Arbor, Michigan

Produced and distributed by
UMI Research Press
an imprint of
University Microfilms International
A Xerox Information Resources Company
Ann Arbor, Michigan 48106

Library of Congress Cataloging in Publication Data

**Ward, Larry Wayne.**
The motion picture goes to war.

(Studies in cinema ; no. 37)
Based on the author's thesis (Ph.D.)—University of
Iowa, 1981.
Includes index.
1. World War, 1914-1918—Motion pictures and the war.
2. Moving-pictures—United States—History—20th century.
I. Title.   II. Series.
D522.23.W37   1985        791.43'09'09358        85-14034
ISBN 0-8357-1683-X (alk. paper)

*For Ann, Mary Ann and Wayne*

# Contents

# List of Illustrations

# Preface

This book grew out of a film. As a graduate student in an innovative cross-disciplinary program in American Cinema/American /Studies at the University of Iowa, I had the opportunity to participate in the production of an hour-long documentary for Post-Newsweek Television and Blackhawk Films. Under the guidance of David Shepard, formerly of Blackhawk Films (now Special Projects Officer for the Directors Guild of America West), and working together with three fellow Iowa graduate students (John Abel, Robert Allen, and Peter Dufour), we produced *The Moving Picture Boys in the Great War,* a compilation film about World War I motion picture propaganda.

While doing research for the film, I became interested in the use of motion pictures by the Committee on Public Information (CPI), the U.S. government's official wartime propaganda agency. Under the leadership of chairman George Creel, the CPI created a Division of Films to exploit the motion picture as a channel for public information and persuasion, the first large-scale attempt by the U.S. government to employ this relatively new medium in an official capacity. By the end of the First World War, the CPI had developed a surprisingly complex and sophisticated motion picture campaign, a program which provided many precedents for the far better-known government film effort in World War II.

Initially, at least, my primary objective was to chronicle and analyze the government's use of motion pictures in the Great War. In his various reports on CPI activities, Creel seemed to generate as many questions as answers, offering only the barest information about the kind of films the CPI produced, and almost nothing about how and where they were made, who made them, and how these films were distributed and exhibited. As I progressed further in my research, however, it became clear that the government's wartime film program was inextricably linked to the contributions of the private film industry.

The government's interest in motion pictures coincided with a period of rapid growth in the American film industry, a period characterized by the introduction of longer and better films, the construction of new "first-run" theaters, the development of powerful studios and stars, and the emergence of a larger and more affluent middle-class audience. Wartime correspondence between industry leaders and government officials, particularly President Woodrow Wilson and George Creel, revealed the film industry's seemingly overwhelming desire to obtain official recognition and approval.

In many respects the industry's quest for acceptance and approval echoes, on a much smaller scale, the central theme of Garth Jowett's wonderful social history of American film, *Film: The Democratic Art.* Less than a decade prior to the First World War, the motion picture was considered a rather disreputable form of amusement, a peepshow novelty suitable chiefly for the uneducated masses. The war, and the government's desire to use motion pictures as part of its wartime public relations campaign, provided the American film industry with a unique opportunity to enhance its stature and solidify its role in American society.

Although contemporary observers made extravagant claims about the effectiveness of the government's World War I film program, most of the work was begun too late in the war to have much impact on public opinion. The great wave of propaganda research generated after the First World War focused, rightly, in my opinion, on the persuasive power of the press. What is important here is that contemporary filmmakers and government officials *thought* motion picture propaganda was effective and that they tried to use motion pictures in this new persuasive role during the First World War.

I have tried to use the word "propaganda" without attaching a negative connotation to it. The modern use of the word is far different from its use during the First World War, when "propaganda" was understood more in its dictionary sense: spreading or extending a doctrine or idea.

There are many people I want to thank for their help and guidance. The Rockefeller Foundation provided a fellowship which helped me begin the research for this book and also to start production on *The Moving Picture Boys in the Great War.* Post-Newsweek Television and Blackhawk Films made it possible to collect and view most of the extant war-related films in the National Archives, the Library of Congress and in private collections. I am also in debt to Dudley Andrew, John Raeburn, Franklin Miller, Robert Pepper and especially Richard MacCann and Larry Gelfand, a consummate American historian.

David Shepard played a far greater role than he realizes in helping to define the scope of this work, and my fellow graduate students at the University of Iowa, John Abel and Bobby Allen, provided many invaluable insights and observations.

Terry Hynes gave hours of careful reading and counsel, and Ed Trotter and George Mastroianni offered the kind of encouragement and prodding that kept the entire project in perspective.

Finally, I would be remiss in not thanking Ann Ward for her encouragement and support. Through hours of proofreading and discussion, I am sure she learned more than she ever wanted about the U.S. government's World War I film program. Her patience and unflagging interest were irreplaceable.

# 1

# Backdrop

If the First World War had occurred just a few years earlier, there would probably have been no reason to write this book. It is doubtful that the motion picture would have been sufficiently developed as a medium of mass entertainment or communication to play a meaningful role in a government film program. Prior to World War I, in fact, the United States government had made only limited use of motion pictures in an official capacity. Several government agencies, notably the Agriculture Department and the Department of the Interior, had begun to make short informational films; but their film production units were small, and their films were not widely distributed. When the Army Signal Corps, for example, wanted to shoot films of a historic test flight by the Wright Brothers in 1908, they were forced to ask the Agriculture Department for assistance. The Signal Corps, it turned out, had neither cameramen nor cameras.[1]

Ten years later this had completely changed. By the end of the First World War, the Photographic Section in the Signal Corps had built a staff of nearly six hundred men, and Signal Corps cameramen had shot almost one million feet of film in Europe and the United States. Some of this film was turned over to the U.S. government's official World War I propaganda agency—the Committee on Public Information (CPI). From this material, the CPI's Division of Films produced over sixty government motion pictures, ranging from multi-reel features like *Pershing's Crusaders* to a weekly newsreel entitled the *Official War Review*.[2]

What was the reason for this change? How and why did the United States government embark on such a large-scale effort to use the young motion picture medium as a channel for public information and persuasion? These are complex questions and we can do little more here than suggest some answers.

The war, obviously, provided most of the impetus for the government's new film program. With the very life of the nation threatened by global conflict, it is hardly surprising that government officials would use any medium to help mobilize public opinion. We should also consider the impact of progressive ideology which emphasized the people's role in government. In the first part of the twentieth century, progressive presidents showed a growing awareness of the importance of public opinion, as well as of their ability to manage it. The administration of Theodore Roosevelt, for example, was marked by increased contact with the press and the use of executive press releases to disseminate news and public information. Woodrow Wilson instituted the first regularly scheduled presidential press conferences. Although Wilson later abandoned this practice, his interest in managing public opinion eventually culminated during the First World War in the Committee on Public Information, which he established (by Executive Order 2594) on April 13, 1917.[3]

Another reason, and perhaps the most important, for the government's establishment of a wartime film effort relates to the rapid growth of the American film industry. Film historians have long pointed to World War I as the period when the motion picture came of age as both an art and an industry. During the war years the film industry experienced a number of developments and innovations which enhanced the motion picture's status as a mass medium and reshaped the American film business as well.[4]

## Coming of Age

The development of the star system, the introduction of feature-length films, and the construction of large first-run "picture palaces" like the Strand Theatre in New York had all started by the beginning of the First World War. The war years also marked the beginning of what Mae Heutig has described as the "vertical integration" of the American film industry, i.e., the combining within a single film company of what had previously been the separate areas of production, exhibition, and distribution.[5]

Production costs escalated on every front. The growing film audience seemed to place more emphasis on complete stories.[6] As a result, film companies increasingly found themselves paying royalties to prominent writers in order to use their books or plays as the bases for films. Such stories, in turn, often raised the costs of production in other areas such as costumes, props and sets. With production costs escalating, it became even more important for film producers to protect their investments by hiring established stars, or by building studio organizations which could produce a steady supply of films and ensure their widest distribution.

Before World War I, the center of film production had been shifting from New York to Hollywood. As the war continued, this trend intensified. The quality of motion pictures improved. Film programs no longer changed on a daily basis. This necessitated the development of new methods for distribution and exhibition. To fill the new theaters with patrons, film companies began to

Figure 1.   Tally's storefront theater was one of the first permanent
movie theaters in the United States.
(Post-Newsweek Television Stations, Inc. and Blackhawk
Films)

Figure 2. Built in 1914, the Strand was the first of the new "movie palaces." (Post-Newsweek Television Stations, Inc. and Blackhawk Films)

expend more effort and money on publicity and advertising. Motion pictures were clearly in the process of becoming both a major mass medium and a far more complex business. Competition within the film industry during the war years reached a level of intensity that historian Lewis Jacobs has described as a sort of mad gold rush, characterized by "... dramatic announcements of new companies, revolutionary policies, fantastic successes or failures."[7]

Most of this growth had no connection with the war, but in the film export business, the Great War had a direct and immediate impact. Before August 1914, European film producers had provided the American film industry with its strongest competition. Two of the original members of the once-powerful Motion Picture Patents Company, Pathe and Melies, had been foreign companies; and many foreign film manufacturers, including Itala, Gaumont, Great Northern, Ambrosio, and Eclair, had New York offices when the war began.[8] The World War had a devastating effect on most of these companies. Vital employees were drafted into the army and European film companies were forced to compete with the military for supplies and equipment needed to make films. Some of the same raw materials used to manufacture film stock were needed for the production of gun powder; and cameras, lenses, and film processing chemicals were also increasingly difficult to obtain.[9]

Prior to the war, London had been the center of world film trade. But the disruption of European film production and the difficulty of shipping films out of many European ports put foreign manufacturers at a great disadvantage. American film companies were quick to capitalize on what one trade magazine gleefully described as "the psychological moment for every branch of the industry."[10]

Although American companies faced the same problems as their European counterparts in shipping films to the continent, they were able to make almost immediate inroads in the British market. The British Board of Trade reported that in the first two months of 1915, American films made up 85 percent of the films imported into Great Britain.[11] Statistics released by the Bureau of Foreign and Domestic Commerce showed that American film exports for the first eight months of 1915 nearly doubled the quantity of films exported during the previous two years.[12] By 1916, American films, valued at ten million dollars, were sent abroad, primarily to England, while only one million dollars worth of foreign films were imported into the United States.[13]

The disruption of European production also enabled American film companies to open up new markets in areas which had previously been controlled by European manufacturers. Writing in 1915 for the trade magazine *Moving Picture World,* W. Stephen Bush could barely contain his excitement about the golden opportunity awaiting American film producers in South America:

> Not a foot of motion picture film is produced in South America. The market must be supplied exclusively by importation. The population of Latin America is greater than that of Germany and as great as that of France and Italy combined. The market is open to all producers on even terms. . . . At present the best grade of film is supplied entirely by European producers. This is the best time to reach out for the South American market. Banking facilities are better than ever before; transportation has been vastly improved; the old prejudice against the Yankee is rapidly dying out and to some extent has disappeared even now.[14]

*Moving Picture World,* in fact, had already taken steps to expand its own Latin American operations. The cornerstone of this effort was the publication of a Spanish-language edition of *Moving Picture World* entitled *Cine-Mundial.* Dr. F.G. Orteyga, a former journalist who had also served with the Cuban delegation in London, was appointed editor of *Cine-Mundial,* and he was assisted by L. H. Allen, a film distributor and exhibitor with considerable experience in the South American market. The publicity campaign for *Cine-Mundial* stressed the "new era of understanding" which the magazine could foster between the two hemispheres, but its primary goal was clearly to help American film companies as they expanded their South American operations.[15]

There is no way to judge the effect of *Cine-Mundial* in the Latin American market, but American film companies did seem to heed the call from south of the border. By 1916 the Fox Film Corporation had established branch offices in Rio de Janeiro, Sao Paulo, Buenos Aires, Rosario, and Montevideo.[16] And later the same year, *Moving Picture World*'s correspondent in Rio de Janeiro filed a glowing report about the success of American films in Brazil:

> What little there is left of French and Italian films in this country proves how complete has become the American invasion of this market. An American who arrives in this city for the first time may make himself at home so far as amusements go, and he may see his favorite actor in almost any of the numerous amusement houses on the "avenue."[17]

The growing domination of American films in the world film market was another sign of the industry's rapid development during the war years. By the end of the war, industry spokesmen were claiming, incorrectly, that the motion picture business had become the fifth largest industry in the United States, a statement which actually reflected the industry's desire to be accorded the press-like status of a "fifth estate."[18] Such inflated claims are understandable. In a short period of time the motion picture had achieved a degree of respectability and acceptance which probably astounded all but the most optimistic early film pioneers. Had the World War occurred just a few years earlier, motion pictures would probably have played nothing more than the limited role they played in the Spanish-American War at the turn of the century. Without the industry's spectacular growth, without the new innovations, it is unlikely that motion pictures would have warranted more than a passing glance from government officials. Certainly, as President Woodrow Wilson discovered, motion pictures were becoming increasingly difficult to ignore.

## Mr. President, See My Film

On February 18, 1915, Woodrow Wilson, his daughter, members of his cabinet and their families gathered in the East Room of the White House to watch David Wark Griffith's twelve-reel Civil War epic, *The Birth of a Nation*. The next night, members of Congress and the Supreme Court, including Chief Justice Edward White, saw the film in the ballroom of the Raleigh Hotel in Washington.[19]

Both of these unprecedented screenings were arranged by Thomas Dixon, a Baptist minister turned novelist, playwright and screenwriter. Dixon had maintained contact with Wilson since his days as a graduate student at Johns Hopkins, and as a personal favor to him, the president agreed to view *The Birth of a Nation* provided projection equipment could be brought to the White House and that there would be no publicity concerning the private screening. Evidently Dixon's command performance was a smashing success. After watching the film, Wilson reportedly said: "It is like writing history in lightning. My only regret is that it is all so terribly true."[20]

This story has been told and retold in most film histories. *The Birth of a Nation* is, after all, one of the most important films in motion picture history. It was the first important American-made feature-length film and signaled the advent of the feature film as the industry's standard unit of production. In addition, Griffith's sensitive use of the camera and his mastery of film editing made a significant contribution to the development of film narrative technique.

But as important as *The Birth of a Nation* was to the development of the motion picture as an art form, the large audiences drawn to the film and the controversy it generated also indicated the medium's potential social and political impact. For many Americans, both black and white, *The Birth of a Nation* represented an intolerable justification of racial bias and white supremacy. When the film opened in Los Angeles in early February 1915, the local branch of the recently formed National Association for the Advancement of Colored People (NAACP) secured a commitment from the mayor to eliminate some of the film's most inflammatory scenes. Eventually the NAACP succeeded in convincing local censorship boards in several cities and states to remove some of the film's more racist sections, and in a few cases, the film was banned entirely from commercial theaters.[21]

These protests, however, did not seem to deter attendance. Audiences throughout the country thronged to the film and less than a month after the White House screening, Dixon told the president that the negative publicity surrounding the film, what he called "valuable abuse," actually seemed to be spurring public interest in the film. [22]

Though Dixon was gloating about the positive effects of negative publicity, the White House was not. At hearings where the NAACP had sought to block the screening of *The Birth of a Nation*, lawyers for the film tried a new line of defense, revealing that both the president and the chief justice of the Supreme Court had seen the film and had found nothing objectionable in it. This implied endorsement angered Justice White in particular. He threatened to publicly denounce the film and wrote Wilson, suggesting that the president make an effort to stop such testimonials. [23] Several weeks later, in response to an inquiry by Representative Thomas C. Thatcher, Joseph Tumulty, Wilson's secretary, tried to clarify the president's involvement with the picture:

> . . . it is true that *The Birth of a Nation* was produced before the President and his family at the White House, but the President was entirely unaware of the character of the play before it was presented and has at no time expressed his approbation of it. Its exhibition at the White House was a courtesy extended to an old acquaintance. [24]

Wilson obviously had many pressing matters on his mind in the spring of 1915, but the controversy aroused by *The Birth of a Nation* surely increased his awareness of the motion picture's growing importance as a medium of mass communication. Throughout the war the president received numerous requests from filmmakers anxious to secure the presidential "imprimatur" for their own films. D. W. Griffith, for example, wrote the president a short time after the White House screening seeking his assistance on a series of historical and political films which he claimed "could be made to sledge hammer home those opinions and thoughts which you might desire to put into the very hearts of the American people." [25] Although the president expressed some interest in Griffith's proposal, he declined any direct involvement, citing the pressures of his busy schedule. [26]

Griffith's desire to involve the president in his new film projects was hardly an isolated incident. Throughout the war years Wilson heard from a variety of filmmakers, producers, studio executives and publicists. There were, of course, many reasons for filmmakers to write the president of the United States, but if there is a single theme which shines through this correspondence, it is the American film industry's almost obsessive desire to secure official recognition and approval. Social historian Robert Sklar has suggested at least one possible motive: the movies were the first medium of

Figure 3.   D. W. Griffith and his brilliant cameraman, Billy Bitzer,
ponder a shot.
(Post-Newsweek Television Stations, Inc. and Blackhawk
Films)

communication controlled by men "who did not share the ethnic or religious backgrounds of the traditional cultural elites."[27] In fact, many of the important early film pioneers like William Fox, Samuel Goldfish (Goldwyn), Carl Laemmle and Adolph Zukor were Eastern European Jews, fairly recent immigrants who had gone from careers in the jewelry or clothing businesses to positions of prominence in the film industry. For them, the Great War may have intensified the motion picture's long-standing cultural inferiority complex, raising new questions about loyalty, patriotism and public service. And, when the war began, the movies were not very far removed from their humble origins in the vaudeville houses, nickelodeons and storefront theaters, a heritage which the Hungarian-born Zukor himself considered a "slum tradition."[28] Against that background it is easier to understand the meeting that the Universal Film Manufacturing Company tried to arrange with Woodrow Wilson so that its German-born president, Carl Laemmle, could simply "shake hands" with the president of the United States.[29]

As trivial as this request may seem, it is symbolic of the acceptance and recognition that many filmmakers sought for themselves and their medium. It would have been flattering of course, and possibly a boost to business, for the president to show interest in any film or film company. But in the years prior to American entry into the First World War, there was still another reason for the president and other government officials to become the focal point of an industry-wide public relations campaign: the threat of government regulation.

Shortly after the war began in the summer of 1914, Congress passed the first of several war-related taxes on motion pictures. A special war tax was enacted in October 1914 as a means of offsetting an expected decline in import duties caused by the European war; it provided for new taxes on loans, alcoholic beverages, and various forms of amusement, including motion picture theaters.[30]

To further alarm the industry, the implementation of federal censorship legislation seemed a distinct possibility. Prior to World War I most attempts to regulate the motion picture industry and motion picture content had taken place on the state or municipal level, but in early 1915 Representative D. M. Hughes (Democrat) of Georgia introduced a bill to establish a federal motion picture commission.[31] Under the terms of Hughes' bill, President Wilson would have been responsible for appointing five motion picture commissioners to examine and license all films before they went into interstate commerce.[32]

Though this legislation was never close to passage, the threat of censorship and the very real burden of war taxes helped unify the motion picture industry. In a business known for its competitiveness and cut-throat individualism, these issues provided a rallying point. Filmmakers and film companies alike were willing to put aside their rivalries in a concentrated effort to educate both the public and government officials about the evils of censorship and taxation.

One sign of this new spirit of unity was the formation of the Motion Picture Board of Trade in September of 1915. The membership of this organization cut across the entire spectrum of industry interests: manufacturers, exhibitors, publishers, suppliers, writers, directors and actors. In an interview with *Moving Picture World,* the Board of Trade's executive secretary, Jacob W. Binder, summarized his new organization's basic objectives:

> We propose to start a campaign of publicity which will provide the press of the country with all the essential facts of the motion picture industry. Our bureau of information will offer its services to the press of the country. In this way we hope to get the truth about motion pictures before the public, to combat prejudice, to conquer ignorance and to diffuse knowledge of the truth. We propose to be heard in the halls of legislation, opposing all unjust and oppressive laws aimed against motion picture interests, but admitting at the same time constructive and beneficial legislation, for we believe that the true interest of the industry and the true interest of the public are identical.[33]

The next year, a similar organization, one which would later make a significant contribution to the U. S. government's wartime film effort, the National Association of the Motion Picture Industry (NAMPI), was formed in New York. William A. Brady was elected president. Although neither of these trade associations survived much beyond the First World War, their representatives made frequent appearances before congressional committees to lobby against censorship and taxation during the war years. These organizations also spearheaded the industry's comprehensive public relations campaign.

Most of this publicity effort was concentrated on Congress and the press, but industry leaders were also anxious to draw the president out on the censorship question. If the Hughes censorship bill had been passed, Wilson would have been responsible for appointing the five members of the Motion Picture Commission. Not surprisingly, the trade associations made a determined effort to elicit the president's views about censorship.

In December 1915, Jacob Binder wrote Wilson, inviting him to speak at the Motion Picture Board of Trade's annual dinner. His letter also provided him with the opportunity to give the president a little sales pitch about the motion picture:

> You may not realize that the motion picture is today one of the greatest forces in the country. As a medium of thought expression it ranks with the press and the spoken word. More than ten million people daily throng the thirteen thousand motion picture theatres throughout the country. As a propaganda medium, it is unexcelled. It speaks a universal language. It speaks convincingly. It is bound to play a tremendously important part in the

next presidential campaign. I want the men who ARE the motion picture industry to know the President of the United States, and to believe in him, his personality and his policies as I do.[34]

The same day Binder also wrote Tumulty, urging him to use his influence to ensure the president's acceptance. With Tumulty, Binder took a different tack, describing in detail the dangers awaiting any politician who failed to recognize the tremendous power of the screen when used "deliberately . . . for political purposes."[35] With obvious relish, Binder explained the fate of Harold J. Mitchell, a candidate for the state legislature of New York:

> Last year he introduced a bill creating a state censor board (another name for political graft harassing the motion picture industry). Through the efforts of the men now constituting the Motion Picture Board of Trade, this bill was defeated. Mitchell ran for re-election. His campaign slogan was "Censor the Movies." The screens in his district ran a single slide opposing the principle of legalized censorship, and not mentioning Mitchell's name. In a district normally Republican by a thousand majority, he was beaten by more than a thousand votes. A Democrat was elected.[36]

Despite Binder's heavy-handed invitation, Wilson agreed to speak at the Board of Trade dinner in the Biltmore Hotel in New York. The movie men were delighted, viewing the presidential visit as a sign of official approval. Plans were made to record the event on film so that it could be shown to the public through the major newsreel services. In an effort to help the president prepare for his speech, Binder wrote him again, enclosing a list of "facts" about the motion picture which provides a remarkable summary of the wishful thinking and self-aggrandizement that characterized the motion picture industry's official public relations campaign:

#### FACTS ABOUT THE MOTION PICTURES

1   It is a NEW VEHICLE OF EXPRESSION
It is akin and similar to
   (a) Speech.
   (b) The printed page in a book.
   (c) The newspaper.
Those who know it best speak of the motion picture as the FIFTH ESTATE. The Constitution expressly guarantees freedom from pre-publicity restraint—censorship— to the spoken and printed word.
THE SAME GUARANTEE SHOULD BE GIVEN TO THIS NEW VEHICLE OF EXPRESSION.

2   The language of the Motion Picture is a UNIVERSAL LANGUAGE.

3   There are in the United States 12,000 motion picture theatres.
12,000,000 people attend these theatres EVERY DAY.

Figure 4.  Frame enlargement from a contemporary newsreel
showing President Wilson marching in a preparedness
parade.
(Post-Newsweek Television Stations Inc. and Blackhawk
Films)

Five hundred million dollars are invested in the industry.
Nearly a million people are employed in it.
The industry has grown to its present place and magnitude in just a little over a decade.

4  There are now six nationally circulated News picture services. These tell in motion
pictures the news of the world. First they were issued only monthly; then weekly; now
twice weekly; soon they will be dailies with two or three editions.[37]

Binder's dream of a major presidential address devoted entirely to the
motion picture was never realized. On January 27, 1916, the president
unveiled his new preparedness program in speeches before the New York
Federation of Churches and the Railway Business Association. At the
conclusion of a patriotic speech to the railway men, Wilson was escorted to the
Board of Trade dinner by a five-hundred man contingent from the Ninth
Coast Guard Artillery.

This entrance might have been good for the newsreel cameras, but the
president clearly had more on his mind than motion pictures. Speaking
extemporaneously, Wilson gave a rambling speech about the political
situation in Mexico. His only reference to the movies was about the newsreels.
Seeing himself on screen, the president revealed, "often sent him to bed
unhappy." Wilson also told the filmmakers that if they could only find some
way of taking pictures of what was going on in his mind, they would find

material "that would be entertaining to any audience anywhere."[38] The president's refusal to seriously address the industry's concerns about censorship must have been a bitter disappointment to both Binder and the Board of Trade, but the Binder-Wilson correspondence does indicate one of the central themes in the industry's official public relations campaign: the attempt to differentiate the functions of the motion picture from other forms of entertainment or communication.

The trade magazine *Moving Picture World* described that difference as the "distinct educational value of the screen," a difference, it argued, which the Italian government had already recognized in its own taxation of motion pictures:

> Motion pictures are taxed in Italy if they deal with purely dramatic themes, but they are exempt from taxation if they are educational in character. A motion picture theater which shows at least one or two educational films (newsreels) on its daily program ought to be exempt from special war taxation. If we tax educational films we might as well tax the newspapers and the books and the lectures in the universities. The motion picture theater is the university of the plain people.[39]

This argument was heard time and again during the war years. Although most of the industry's resources were devoted to the production of theatrical films, the newsreels played an increasingly special role in the industry's official public relations effort. In an effort to counter charges that the movies had a negative impact on social and moral standards, industry spokesmen began to stress the educational benefits that the American people derived from the screen. While some filmmakers undoubtedly felt that their dramatic films provided a form of education for the masses, it was often easier to justify claims that the movies were "educational and informative" by focusing attention on the newsreels.

President Wilson, in fact, was well acquainted with the newsreels. He had begun hearing from the newsreel companies shortly after his inauguration in 1913. At that time, the newsreel companies were primarily interested in securing pictures of Wilson and his cabinet, or in obtaining permission to photograph the wedding of Wilson's daughter.[40] Although the president showed some interest in these proposals, he was fearful that the White House might be overrun by cameramen, and he limited his personal involvement to the filming of public events.

In March of 1915, however, Carl Laemmle, president of the Universal Film Manufacturing Company, devised a novel plan for coaxing Wilson into participating in a special issue of Universal's *Animated Weekly* newsreel. Laemmle wrote the president, trying to convince him that Universal's newsreel offered a unique means of communicating directly with the American public. What Laemmle had in mind was a presidential message copied on film which could be shown in movie theaters across the nation. Citing the movies' "tremendous influence on the public," and the "30 million people in the United States who view pictures every day," Laemmle urged Wilson to take advantage of this powerful new communications medium:

> Think of the amount of good you will accomplish by sending a message of good cheer to the American public at this time. The subject is entirely in your hands. We would like to have it on optimism. You can preach the gospel of neutrality if your prefer or stimulate interest in home industry. There is some message that you want to send to the American public; will you let us send it for you?[41]

There is no record of presidential action on this request, but by December of 1915, Laemmle had begun gathering similar messages from other prominent people to be used in conjunction with a special New Year's release of the *Animated Weekly*. Each person's statement was to be shown on the screen via title cards, preceded by a short piece of film which portrayed the author in some characteristic pose. Laemmle wrote Wilson again, trying to secure his participation in the project, but the president declined, noting that "composing messages of this sort has always been the particular sort of thing I did not know how to do."[42]

Laemmle, however, was not used to taking no for an answer, even from the chief executive. He wrote his own version of a presidential New Year's message and then asked the president by telegram if he could use that version in the newsreel. As a clinching argument, he also let the president know that he had already obtained similar messages from the president's entire cabinet, and from many others, including John D. Rockefeller, J. P. Morgan, German Ambassador Johann von Bernstorff, and British Ambassador Cecil Spring Rice.[43] This last bit of news was evidently all that the president needed. He immediately rewrote Laemmle's draft and made his first contribution to the Universal newsreel:

> I sincerely join with my fellow citizens in praying that God may grant unto us during the year 1916 the blessings of abundant and rewarding prosperity, and that He may give us as a nation the guidance we need in playing the very difficult role we are now endeavoring to play amidst the confused affairs of a world dominated by war. In maintaining our position as the foremost neutral nation in the world we must not only guide our government wisely, but must ourselves as individual citizens seek to attain that high standard of individual justice and probity which has been the ideal of the nation from the day of its independence. God grant that the American people may continue to enjoy peace and that they may presently see its blessings return to all the other nations of the world. I wish all a very happy New Year.[44]

During the 1916 election campaign, the idea of using screen messages of this kind was frequently discussed. In March, Wilson heard from Edward L.

Fox of Paramount Pictures, who described the advantage of using motion pictures to show the "big things" the president was doing for the country. Like most people trying to convince Wilson to use motion pictures, Fox stressed the large crowds attracted to the movies. He also introduced a new argument about screen publicity, the advantages of addressing what was essentially a captive theater audience. In comparison to a magazine reader, Fox assured the president, a film viewer could not turn the page on motion picture propaganda—"no matter how prejudiced he may be on a certain subject."[45]

At first Wilson seemed intrigued with Fox's idea and he instructed Tumulty to inform Fox that he would dictate some sentences for him "at the earliest possible moment."[46] Wilson evidently neglected to follow up on this offer and when he heard from Fox again, he told Tumulty that Fox should simply "cull what he needs" out of speeches that he had given in the past.[47]

At almost the same time, Wilson heard from William Brady, president of the National Association of the Motion Picture Industry. Brady, a staunch Democrat and active Wilson supporter, had maintained close contact with the president during the industry's continuing battle against federal censorship and war taxes.[48] Working together with Henry Morgenthau of the Democratic National Committee, Brady had developed a plan for exploiting screen publicity nearly identical to the one already proposed by Paramount's Edward Fox:

> ... if the President would agree to make several simple speeches—kindergarden [*sic*] ones I would call them—on Peace, Prosperity, or any of the slogans of the campaign, with personal views of the President, portions of his speech could be shown on the screen between views of him.
>
> For instance, if he spoke on Peace, we could show in the picture the horrors of war. If he spoke on Prosperity, we could show pictures of mills, mines and farms throughout the United States at the present time enjoying the limit of happiness and prosperous welfare.[49]

While plans of this kind may have intrigued the president, his frequent contact with the movie men had also made him aware of some very real problems with using motion pictures for political purposes. While acknowledging the "very considerable advantages" of screen publicity, Wilson wondered how he could work with one motion picture company and keep its competitors from charging him with favoritism.[50] Another problem was inherent in the silent motion picture. The industry's practice of showing scenes of a speaker interspersed with title cards explaining what the speaker was saying was awkward at best. To a speaker with Wilson's oratorical skills, the limitations of performing speeches before a silent camera must have seemed almost unbearable. Although there was no way to entirely avoid employing this technique, the president did express some serious doubts abouts its value:

It is just the simple fact that I do not know how to lend myself to plans of this sort. The speeches will be flat and my self-consciousness in the face of the camera will make the whole thing awkward and ineffective. I ought, perhaps, to apologize to the campaign managers for being so unserviceable, but the simple fact is as I have stated it.[51]

One novel solution to this problem was supplied by S. A. Bloch, an enterprising filmmaker-inventor from Chicago. Bloch claimed to have perfected a talking-motion picture apparatus and he tried to convince the president that his new invention was the perfect tool for delivering campaign speeches to spellbound movie audiences. The basic advantage of talking pictures, as Bloch described them, was that "the speaker is always in good voice; on time; and full of magnetism."[52] Bloch's "new" invention, a record player mechanically attached to a projector, was actually an old idea. As early as 1889, Thomas Edison and his assistant W. K. L. Dickson had experimented with film projected in rough synchronization with Edison's phonograph cylinders. Although Bloch's process may have been technically feasible in 1916, the means of amplifying the sound had not yet been developed and it never seemed to have crossed Bloch's mind that installing such a system in a significant number of commercial movie theaters would have been an expensive and time-consuming process. In any case, Bloch's scheme held no appeal for the president. Evidently, the president had made some sound recordings a few years earlier, and he told Tumulty in no uncertain terms that it had been "a dismal failure and I don't mean to try it again."[53]

Ironically, the one film which may actually have had some impact on public opinion during the 1916 campaign was neither an official campaign film nor a newsreel, but a theatrical film—Thomas Ince's pacifist war drama—*Civilization*. This film told the story of a submarine captain who refused to sink an unarmed passenger liner. After being sent home, the captain embarks on a campaign to convince his king and fellow countrymen that they should pursue peace instead of war. He is thrown in jail and dies, only to be reincarnated in the body of Christ. In this spirit-form, he confronts the king and leads him on a tour of battlefields in his war-torn country, forcing the king to see the horrors of war with his own eyes. Deeply moved, the king eventually signs a peace treaty and returns his subjects to their blissful prewar state of peace and happiness.[54]

As melodramatic as this might sound, *Civilization* did seem to echo Wilson's 1916 campaign slogan: "He kept us out of war." According to William Cochrane, a press representative for the Democratic National Committee, *Civilization* played a significant role in Wilson's re-election, a perception which might have been enhanced by the fact that some prints of the film contained an epilogue in which the president was actually shown shaking hands with producer Ince and congratulating him on the film.[55]

This on-screen presidential endorsement was probably produced without Wilson's knowledge. It was a publicity scheme cooked up by Ince's energetic publicity manager, Alec Lorimotz. After seeing *Civilization* at a local Washington theater, Wilson had written Ince several times, praising the film and thanking him for his "efforts to advance the cause which I have the honor to represent at this moment."[56] A few months later, long after the film had gone into distribution, Ince obtained permission to shoot film of Wilson at some public event at Shadow Lawn. On his own initiative, Lorimotz copied a few of Wilson's positive comments about the film onto title cards and cut them together with footage of Ince and Wilson together at Shadow Lawn. Lorimotz then began attaching this short trailer to prints of *Civilization,* where, as he later assured the president, it always "received a wonderful reception."[57]

In the end, however, there was a great deal more talk about campaign films than action. Not to be left out, the Republican National Committee commissioned an official campaign film from the Hal Reid Photoplay Company. But when the film was finished it showed scenes of the president asleep at his desk and of rebels attacking Catholic nuns in Mexico, and the Republicans refused to sanction it.[58]

The filmmakers and film companies were clearly more impressed with the potential of screen publicity than either political party. Citing the advantages of addressing a "captive audience" and quoting inflated movie attendance figures, the movie men continued to bombard the president with a variety of schemes for using motion pictures to communicate with the American people. While the camera-shy president did expand his contact with the newsreel companies, allowing somewhat greater coverage of White House activities,[59] he never agreed to employ motion pictures directly in his re-election campaign.

Nevertheless, the rapid growth of the American film industry and the threat of government regulation brought the film industry into much closer contact with the president and other government officials. Filmmakers who just a few years earlier had been embarrassed to be associated with the fledgling film business now corresponded directly with the White House. In the battle against film censorship and war taxes, industry leaders had become regulars in the halls of Congress. Equally important was the development of personal relationships such as the one between President Wilson and William Brady of the NAMPI. Ironically, the industry's new trade associations, organizations which were created primarily to lobby against government interference, actually facilitated the government's use of the motion picture industry later in the war.

To some extent, the film industry may have become a prisoner of its own publicity. Having stressed so strongly the motion picture's unique power to persuade and inform, the industry may have been under some pressure to demonstrate this ability. Despite the president's personal reticence to use motion pictures for political purposes, the two and one-half years of American neutrality provided the perfect testing ground for the concept of screen propaganda.

# 2

# Film and Politics in the Neutrality Years

Before 1914, motion pictures had seldom done anything more than provide entertainment. Although American film companies consistently trumpeted the "informational and educational" value of their newsreels, the newsreels were actually more of an entertainment vehicle than a source of news. In part, the technology of filmmaking worked against the coverage of fast-breaking events. An important story shot in France had to be processed, edited, and shipped across the Atlantic before it could appear in American movie theaters, a time-consuming procedure which explains, at least in part, the newsreel's propensity for more timeless stories—"news" with a long shelf-life: fashion shows, zoo tours, daredevil stunts, new inventions and biographies of the rich, the famous, the unusual. Nevertheless, the First World War and the government's desire to employ motion pictures as a means of public information and persuasion raised new questions about the motion picture's role, or its potential role, in American society. These questions are interesting not only for what they reveal about the growth of the American film industry, but for the tensions they exposed within both the government and the film industry concerning the development of motion picture propaganda.

Today, when the president of the United States is a former film star, moving images are used daily to sell everything from soap flakes to defense budgets. It is no great revelation that press conferences and political conventions are staged with an eye for the camera. Armed with a large staff of pollsters and professional publicity men, politicians regularly use the media to explain their ideas or to promote themselves as candidates. We may not even remember the candidate's name, but we can often recall some of the images from the campaign film: the would-be president walking alone in the surf at sunset, or the candidate, dressed in blue jeans and work shirt, kneeling down in a cornfield to examine the soil. Before the advent of television, when the motion picture was a relatively young medium, the idea of using films to explain policy, to generate public support, to sell war bonds or to encourage enlistment was still new and untested.

This began to change during the two and one-half years of American neutrality in the Great War. From 1914 to 1917, American film audiences had numerous opportunities to see films partial to the Allies or the Central Powers, as well as a variety of films portraying the joys of peace or the dangers of pacifism. Although the United States government made only a limited attempt to use motion pictures during this period, prewar propaganda films provided a number of precedents for the government when it later developed its wartime film program. By the time America entered the war virtually every technique for producing or exploiting screen propaganda had already been tried. During the neutrality years motion pictures were regularly used for the first time on a large scale as a persuasive weapon.

## Newsreels and Neutrality

When the war began in the summer of 1914, most Americans could not envision a reason for American involvement. The European conflict did not appear to threaten interests vital to the United States. More importantly, the broad expanse of the Atlantic Ocean seemed to provide a natural buffer against the flames of foreign battlefields. President Wilson summed up many of these feelings both in his official neutrality proclamation and in a series of policy statements in which he sought to explain non-intervention to the American public. Perhaps the highlight of Wilson's neutrality campaign was a statement he gave to the press on August 18, 1914, in which he urged the nation to "be impartial in thought as well as action . . . ."[1]

The public response to war-related newsreels in the early days of the war demonstrated the difficulty of maintaining this posture, and inadvertently involved the president in a scheme to communicate his neutrality message directly to American film audiences.

The concept of releasing a weekly film "magazine" or newsreel had originated in Europe with the founding of the *Pathe Journal* in Paris. The Pathe Company was also responsible for the first American newsreel, the *Pathe Weekly,* which began releasing issues in the United States in 1911. By August of 1914, however, the *Pathe Weekly* had attracted a bevy of competitors including the *Vitagraph Monthly of Current Events,* the *Mutual Weekly,* the *Hearst-Selig News Pictorial* and the *Universal Animated Weekly.*[2] When the war began these companies seemed to have declared their own war in an effort to satisfy the great public demand for war newsreels. The motion picture trade papers of August were filled with advertisements set in the form of newspaper extras—headlines proclaming "War! War! War!," and in somewhat smaller type, a list of current news releases. Mysterious film companies appeared overnight with equally mysterious news film compilations such as *With Serb and Austrian* or *The Man of the Hour, Kaiser*

*Wilhelm II,* a film which the Kaiser Film Company felt compelled to advertise as "taken from Actual Life and by special permission of the Kaiser himself."[3]

Most of these films were little more than re-edited newsreels, focusing primarily on training activities, equipment displays and endless scenes of marching troops. Actual combat footage was extremely rare, but American audiences thronged to the theaters anyway, anxious for a glimpse of the competing armies and the newest military hardware.

The demand for such "war films" appears to have been greatest in areas where recent immigrants made up a significant part of the population. Most of these new immigrants had settled in large metropolitan areas such as New York and Chicago where they not only supported a thriving foreign language press, but made up a significant part of the early film audience.[4] Not only were the movies inexpensive entertainment for them, but the broad acting style and simple stories were readily accessible to recent immigrants, regardless of their ability to read title cards.[5] In 1914, however, the movies threatened to inflame old rivalries.

In the early months of the war there was a growing fear that the exhibition of war newsreels might lead to violence. Observing the large crowds outside a New York theater, a *Times* reporter warned that "unless the local authorities take some steps to curtail the activities of some film exhibitors, I am afraid we will have riots on the east side before the war is over."[6] Riots, in fact, had already occurred in San Francisco between French and German reservists who were attending the showing of a theatrical film about the Franco-Prussian conflict.[7] Against this background, the National Board of Censorship—an industry-sponsored organization which later became the National Board of Review—issued an appeal to film producers and theater owners:

> When you are producing pictures containing war scenes please precede the actual pictures with about five feet of captions asking the audience to kindly refrain from any expressions of partisanship as the pictures are shown. You will strengthen such an announcement very materially by adding that this request is directly in line with the policy of President Wilson.[8]

In September 1914 Secretary of State William Jennings Bryan happened to attend a theater where the management had followed this recommendation and preceded its newsreels with a request to the audience to refrain from partisan applause. It occurred to Bryan that a similar request copied on film in the president's own handwriting might have a greater impact. Moreover, as Bryan told Wilson, it would explain the need for neutrality to an audience very much in need of such a message. The president complied with Bryan's suggestion and in a short time his letter had been copied on film and was appearing in movie theaters across the nation.[9]

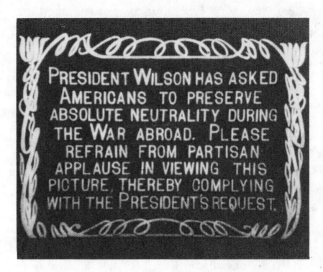

Figure 5.  Wilson's neutrality statement could be copied on movie
film or used as a slide before the newsreel.
(Post-Newsweek Television Stations, Inc. and Blackhawk
Films)

The president's campaign for screen neutrality also received the full
support of the Universal Film Manufacturing Company. In September of
1914, Universal notified the White House that it had produced a short film
entitled *Be Neutral* "in appreciation of the efforts which the President is
making to keep America neutral in the European war."[10] This film was
reportedly produced in forty-eight hours as a means of publicizing Wilson's
neutrality proclamation. It told the story of factory workers who became
embroiled in a heated argument about the war and in the process, let their
factory burn to the ground. In case viewers missed the point of this short
parable, it was supplemented by title cards which said: "Don't Take Sides,"
"Be American First," and "Forget the Horrors of War."[11] Universal also
began running Wilson's neutrality letter with its *Animated Weekly* newsreel,
although Universal's Jack Cohn requested another presidential letter which
was "not quite so long."[12]

In many respects the campaign for neutrality at the newsreels typified the
administration's half-hearted involvement with motion pictures in the
neutrality years. The president did, at the urging of Secretary of State Bryan,
use motion pictures (or motion picture theaters) to amplify his neutrality
proclamation, but the impetus for this campaign was clearly the industry's:
with federal film censorship already under discussion, the last thing the
industry needed was riots at local movie theaters. Even though government

officials had not asked for help, it made sense for the industry to volunteer, not only to head off a possibly dangerous situation, but as a means of demonstrating both the industry's ability and willingness to actively support administration policy.

By modern standards it is difficult to see how this early newsreel coverage could have been considered inflammatory. Authentic scenes of the European conflict were rare and some companies tried to satisfy the demand for "war films" by releasing war-related fictional films. Others simply reached into their film vaults for old newsreel footage of anything that marched or wore a helmet. The *Pathe Weekly* of August 5, 1914, was typical of this early "war coverage." This issue showed stock footage of Emperor Franz Joseph in Paris, King George the Fifth in London, Czar Nicholas II in St. Petersburg, and Kaiser Wilhelm II in Berlin.[13] Other supposedly war-related newsreels gave American audiences a glimpse of Swiss Army maneuvers or scenes of New Jersey governor James Fiedler reviewing national guard troops.[14]

It soon became obvious to almost everyone that the newsreel companies were having a difficult time obtaining actual war films. Archive footage could be passed off as newsreels for only so long and strict military censorship in Europe dampened the prospects of shooting new film of the competing armies. Even if an enterprising newsreel cameraman overcame these obstacles, his problems had just begun. Military authorities were generally reluctant to allow civilian photographers near the front, not only to protect them from the potential danger of enemy fire, but as a means of restricting the release of photographs and newsreels for security reasons. Although a few newsreel companies succeeded in smuggling small amounts of film out of Europe, contemporary accounts provided a stream of horror stories about cameramen who were shot at or arrested as spies, with their equipment confiscated and their film destroyed.[15]

Faced with a seemingly insatiable demand for war films, unscrupulous film producers found a far easier and safer method of giving the public what they thought it wanted. Armed with a few guns, some actors, old uniforms, and a willing cameraman, such producers could easily create stirring "war films" that exceeded the quality of films that could actually be shot in the field. In the early days of the war this practice became so widespread that Universal's J. D. Tippett concluded that "anything you see in America of any consequence is fake," a perception enhanced by exposés about fake war films which appeared in a number of magazines.[16] *The Literary Digest,* for example, obviously enjoyed the opportunity to describe the Hollywood-style production of British "war films":

As the charging "Germans reach the opposite bank and make straight for the "British" machine guns, terrible explosions occur. . . . At the proper moment the fake mines are

Figure 6.   Staging "war films" in Van Courtland Park, New Jersey.
(Post-Newsweek Television Stations, Inc. and Blackhawk
Films)

exploded by throwing a switch or pressing a button, thus sending clouds of smoke and a
dummy figure or two into the air.[17]

## The "Official Films"

The development of what came to be known as "official films" provided an
important means of combatting the general belief that all war pictures were
fake. The term "official films" was used in many ways during the neutrality
period. In the beginning, "official films" were simply films which had been
obtained with the official sanction of either the government or the military in
one of the European nations. Such films might have been purchased from
military cinematographers, or shot by commercial newsreel cameramen under
the watchful eye of military advisors. Although these films seldom featured
battlefield action, the fact that they had been secured "officially" gave
American audiences some assurance that the films they were watching had not
been staged, that what they were seeing were authentic views of armies, tanks,
and on occasion, battlefields. Even the knowledge that such "official films"
had been subject to heavy military censorship tended to increase their
legitimacy. By the middle of 1915, in fact, most of the warring nations had
begun to produce their own "official films." Utilizing photographers and film
editors attached to the military, these government-sponsored productions

offered an unusually vivid means of explaining the war effort to movie audiences both at home and abroad.

Surprisingly, neither the established newsreel companies, nor the warring nations were the first to exploit the concept of "official films." That honor belonged to the *Chicago Tribune* and its two resourceful cameramen, Edwin F. Weigle and Donald D. Thompson. In 1914 and 1915, the *Tribune* released a series of war newsreels including *On the Belgian Battlefield,* perhaps the first "official film," *With the Russians at the Front,* and *The German Side of the War,* probably the first news film exhibited in the United States which showed the war from the German point of view.[18] When war was declared, Weigle and Joseph Patterson, a *Tribune* editor, had sailed for Europe. Both Weigle and Thompson, a freelance photographer-cinematographer, were in Antwerp when the city fell to the Germans. After securing permission to shoot film from the appropriate military authorities, the cameramen shot footage on both sides of the line in Belgium. Later, they continued their work in Germany, with Thompson concentrating his efforts on the Eastern Front where he shot most of the footage for the *Tribune's With the Russians at the Front.*[19] In addition to shooting their own film, both cameramen were able to buy footage from military photographers attached to the participating armies. Often they were required to donate prints of film they had shot to the archives of the host government, a procedure which meant that footage shot by Weigle and Thompson might have appeared in "official" German, French, or British films released later in the United States.[20]

In many respects Thompson and Weigle set the standards for newsreel coverage of the war. Even with official permission to shoot film, their work was often dangerous. Thompson, in particular, seems to have cultivated the image of the death-defying war cameraman, willing to risk all for a few priceless feet of film. According to Alexander Powell of the *New York World,* Thompson's exploits on the battlefield had made him something of a war hero. At the very least, Thompson knew how to dress the part:

> Of all the horde of adventurous characters who were drawn to the Continent on the outbreak of war . . . I doubt if there was a more picturesque figure than a little photographer from Kansas named Donald Thompson. I met him first while paying a flying visit to Ostend. He blew into the consulate there wearing an American army shirt, a pair of British officer's riding breeches, French putees, and a Highlander's forage-cap, and carrying a camera the size of a parlor phonograph. No one but an American could have accomplished what he had, and no one but one from Kansas. He had not only seen the war, all military prohibitions to the contrary, but he had actually photographed it.[21]

When the *Tribune* released its first "official film" in the United States in late 1914, it announced that half of the profits from *On the Belgian Battlefield* would be turned over to the Belgian Red Cross, a procedure which became fairly commonplace when "official films" were exhibited in the United States during the neutrality period.[22] Aligning the film with the American Red Cross had some obvious public relations benefits. Each screening of the film became something more than a night at the movies; it became an opportunity to attend and participate in a gala Red Cross benefit screening. In addition, the Red Cross' involvement provided an aura of neutrality which tended to protect film companies from complaints that their films favored either the Germans or the Allies. Who, after all, could complain about patriotic excesses in the theater when money was being raised for an obviously humanitarian cause?

The *Tribune*'s success with *On the Belgian Battlefield* demonstrated something more. In early December 1914 the *Tribune* presented a $10,000 check to Dr. Cyrille Vermeren, the Belgian consul in Chicago. This was only the first installment of Red Cross contributions generated by *On the Belgian Battlefield* and it showed that war films could be very useful in fundraising.[23]

When the *Tribune* released the feature-length *The German Side of the War* in September 1915, it continued the pattern of benefit screenings by announcing that a share of the film's profits would be donated to a special fund for wounded German soldiers. This film was composed of footage shot by Thompson, Weigle and others, and although the film was advertised as presenting the German point of view, the filmmakers tried to emphasize its neutrality. Thompson's description of *The German Side of the War* was meant to offend no one:

> If you had been with me in Germany and had seen the German soldiery, the wonderful discipline, the endless preparation . . . you would have said: "The whole world can't whip them." But then, if you had been on the other side with me and could have seen the bravery of the English, the enthusiasm of the French, the courage of the Belgians and the great organization of the allies you would have said again: "They can't be whipped."[24]

When *The German Side of the War* opened at the 44th Street Theater in New York it drew record breaking crowds. In the long lines outside the theater, ticket scalpers tricked German-speaking patrons into buying worthless soda tickets. Eventually, extra police had to be called out to avert a riot. The film sold out for every performance, and according to the *Times,* the audience's frenzied reaction to scenes of the kaiser "could not have been outdone had every seat been taken by reservists."[25]

## The German Film Effort

The success of the *Tribune*'s "official films" did not go unnoticed. The Germans were the first of the warring nations to allow cameramen from neutral countries to shoot film with their troops and until the Allies relaxed their ban on newsreel cameramen, the Germans enjoyed a great propaganda advantage. Ironically, the Germans' initial success with "official films" shot by neutral cameramen appears to have undercut efforts to establish a covert German film program in the United States.

As early as March 1915, the German secretary of foreign affairs, Alfred Zimmerman, had recommended the establishment of an organization in the United States to distribute German propaganda films and photographs. This suggestion was put into operation a month later with the incorporation in New York of the American Correspondent Film Company. Felix Malitz was appointed vice-president and general manager and Dr. Albert Feuhr became secretary.[26]

From its inception, the American Correspondent Film Company proved a disappointing venture for the German government. Malitz and Feuhr began their work with a simple and, in the commercial film business, contradictory policy: making money with their films was less important than getting them shown to the largest possible audiences in the very best commercial theaters. While such objectives are understandable in a propaganda campaign, they did not take into account the tremendous expense of booking first-run movie theaters or the high cost of financing an advertising campaign to help fill those theaters with patrons. Throughout its brief existence the American Correspondent Film Company was teetering on the edge of financial disaster.[27]

The company's financial problems were compounded by the difficulty of securing authentic German war films. When the American Correspondent Film Company began operation, Malitz possessed a few films about German culture and industry, and several Austrian war films, most notably Albert K. Dawson's *The Battle of Przemysl*, a four-reel film which highlighted the Austro-Hungarian drive through Galicia on the Eastern Front.[28] The British naval blockade made it extremely difficult to import additional German war films into the United States. In an effort to solve this problem, Malitz made arrangements with the stewards on several neutral Norwegian ocean liners to smuggle films and photographs past the blockade. Next Malitz tried to work out a distribution agreement with the Hearst-newsreel organization, an arrangement which might have made it easier to get films past the British. When that plan fell through, Malitz was able to line up a New York distributor to handle all films supplied by the American Correspondent Film Company.[29]

These plans, however, were doomed. Malitz's negotiations with American film distributors had been contingent on two bases: first, that he could guarantee a steady supply of German war films; and secondly, that he could give a distributor a complete monopoly on official German war films in the United States. Malitz was unable to deliver on either count. He was never able to secure a consistent supply of German war films. Even more damaging was the fact that the German government was unwilling to give the American Correspondent Film Company complete control of German films in the American market.[30]

The German government had been delighted by the positive public reaction to the *Chicago Tribune*'s "official films" and during 1915 and 1916, it granted a number of private companies permission to shoot films of various German military campaigns: *How Germany Makes War* (Central Film Company), *Behind the Fighting Lines of the German Army* (Great Northern), *Germany on the Firing Lines* (Kulee Features), and *The Fighting Germans* (Mutual Film Company). German officials felt that films produced by neutral American companies would have a greater impact on American audiences than films released through a company connected with the German government.

In fact, the relationship between the American Correspondent Film Company and the German propaganda service became common knowledge in August 1915 when the *Chicago Tribune* and the *New York World* published a series of articles based on the stolen papers of German Counselor Henrich Albert. These articles provided a detailed account of the German Information Service in the United States, including the German government's support of the American Correspondent Film Company.[31] When confronted with these revelations Malitz did not deny his relationship with the German government. Instead, he stressed the fact that the American Correspondent Film Company's films had always been openly advertised as "official German films," and that he had always conducted the company's affairs "in a straight-forward, businesslike and neutral manner."[32]

Despite this setback Malitz continued making plans. By March 1916 he had concocted his most grandiose scheme for exploiting German propaganda films in the United States. He tried to convince German officials that they should purchase fifteen large metropolitan motion picture theaters. This, Malitz argued, would allow the German government to shows its films at a profit in choice theaters. After the war, these same theaters would provide a natural outlet for German films in the United States.[33]

By the summer of 1916 the German government had evidently given up on Malitz. The American Correspondent Film Company was disbanded; however, privately produced pro-German films continued to be shown in the United States. In fact, a film entitled *Germany and Its Armies of Today* was playing at the prestigious Strand Theater in New York as late as January 1917.[34]

From the outset the German's covert film effort had been crippled by lack of money and poor organization. Undoubtedly, the most successful pro-German films shown in the United States were actually produced by American companies who either shot their own films or purchased film footage from German military photographers. Compared to that of the Allies, the German film effort was at great disadvantage, a situation Dr. Albert Feuhr tried to explain to his own government:

> Our opponents now seem to have recognized the effectiveness of this propaganda and are exhibiting films from their fronts here which do not fail to make an impression, with extraordinary outlays for expensive advertising, and under the patronage of the highest personalities. Some of the films are quite excellent, others are obviously "maneuver pictures," which, however, have a thrilling effect on the public.[35]

## The Allied Film Effort

Dr. Feuhr's analysis of Allied film activity was hardly an exaggeration. British control of the shipping lanes facilitated the importation of Allied films. Once in the country, Allied films were distributed by companies that were already well established in the United States when the war began: Pathe and Melies distributed most of the French films; the General Film Company, the Motion Picture Patent Company's film distributing subsidiary, eventually provided an outlet for both British and Italian war films.

In the summer of 1915 the French War Department announced the creation of a special film office to coordinate the work of army cinematographers and the three largest private film companies. This office was responsible for producing the first two "official" French films, *France in Arms* and *Fighting in France*. The powerful Pathe Company distributed both of these films when they reached the United States.[36]

The French also began to experiment with new uses for the motion picture. The French commander-in-chief, Joseph Joffre, announced his intention to shoot motion pictures as a means of documenting battles for future historians. In Paris the Ministry of Foreign Affairs began showing films to neutral journalists to combat what it considered misleading German battlefield accounts, and the Ministry of Finance initiated a scheme to use motion pictures to drum up support for the French war loan drive.[37]

When *Fighting in France* appeared in Canada under the sponsorship of the *Toronto World*, Canadian military authorities unveiled another new way to use motion pictures in the war effort—turning movie theaters into mini-recruiting stations. Between reel changes during the film, army recruiters gave patriotic speeches and showed slides of military life. Outside the theater, automobiles were waiting to take interested patrons to the nearest enlistment office.[38]

By 1916 motion pictures had become an important tool in fostering Franco-American relations. One of the most successful "official films," *Our American Boys in the European War*, was actually produced by the American Triangle Company with additional footage supplied by French military cinematographers. This film highlighted the activities of the American Ambulance Corps in France and the Franco-American Flying Corps.[39]

At the New York premiere of *Our American Boys in the European War,* Robert Bacon, the former ambassador to France, followed what was a fairly well-established pattern by announcing that all proceeds from the film would be donated to the American Ambulance Corps in France.[40] To help publicize the film, Triangle arranged a number of special screenings at fashionable resorts and first-run theaters across the country. Triangle also began securing endorsements for *Our American Boys in the European War.* Theodore Roosevelt missed the film's New York premiere, but Triangle wisely arranged a special screening for the former president at its New York office. After watching the film, Roosevelt delivered to the press exactly the kind of rousing endorsement that Triangle was expecting:

> ... these young men whose deeds we have been watching in this film today have been helping this nation save its soul, and, as a whole, the nation has been thinking of saving everything except its soul. The nation has been preaching "safety first"; these boys have been thinking of the soul first. There isn't an American worth calling such who isn't under a heavy debt to these boys for what they have done.[41]

*Our American Boys in the European War* proved to be a natural fund-raiser with American audiences. On December 23, 1916, a special benefit performance of the film sold out the 3,000 seat Strand Theater in New York. Tickets for this screening were priced at five dollars per seat with some boxes selling for one hundred dollars. In addition to the box office receipts, over $36,000 was pledged to the Ambulance Corps during the performance.[42]

The British were somewhat slower than the French to develop a formal motion picture campaign. Wellington House, the British wartime propaganda bureau, was unable to convince the War Office and the Admiralty of the need to utilize motion picture propaganda until the fall of 1915. Charles Urban, who had been actively campaigning for British propaganda films since early in the war, was picked to organize the film effort.[43] Urban's background made him an ideal choice for spearheading the British film campaign. He was an American who had become a naturalized British subject and he had strong ties with the film business on both sides of the Atlantic. He had helped found the *Warwick Chronicle,* an early British newsreel, and the American-owned Charles Urban Trading Company was well known in the U.S. for its "Kinemacolor" newsreels, a process using black and white film and colored filters to produce very primitive color film.[44]

Urban's first film, *Britain Prepared* (known in the United States as *How Britain Prepared*), was not ready for exhibition until March 1916. The film showed scenes of the Grand Fleet in action, a variety of military training activities, and a tour of munitions factories and shipyards. The Patriot Film

Company, an American company with strong British ties, was formed to distribute the film. Using the now familiar pattern for publicizing the film, Urban set up special screenings of *How Britain Prepared* for leaders of the American preparedness movement and various military officials.[45]

Urban also lined up endorsements from Secretary of War Newton D. Baker, and the assistant secretary of the Navy and future president, Franklin D. Roosevelt, who felt that *How Britain Prepared* conveyed a vital message about preparedness to the American people:

> These pictures must be of tremendous interest all over the country and will undoubtedly carry the lesson that, while an enormous amount of work had been done by England since the war began, all of this would have been very greatly simplified if there had been more adequate preparation for it before hostilities commenced.[46]

Even with such positive endorsements, Urban had a difficult time securing adequate bookings for *How Britain Prepared.* The Patriot Film Corporation had disbanded by the time he finished his next "official British war film," *The Battle of the Somme.* This new film was actually part of a fourteen-reel newsreel serial which the British released in four large feature-length blocks including: *The Battle of the Somme, Jellicoe's Grand Fleet, Kirchener's Great Army* and *The Munitions Makers.*[47] These films received a tremendous boost in circulation with the creation of Official Government Pictures, Incorporated, a new company created with the expressed purpose of using films to raise money for the British Relief Fund and the American Field Ambulance Service. Official Government Pictures worked out a simple solution to Urban's distribution problems—they secured an agreement with the General Film Company to handle distribution of British and Italian war films in the United States, a move which ensured Allied war films of regular screenings in movie theaters throughout the country.[48]

Together with the official French war films and a few belated Italian productions like *The Italian Battlefront* and *Italy's Flaming Front,* the sheer volume of Allied motion pictures overwhelmed the German film effort. Although the Germans had been the first major power to recognize the potential of motion picture propaganda, it did not take the Allies very long to take advantage of vastly superior distribution outlets and advertising campaigns. Certainly by the time the United States entered the war in April 1917, official Allied war films assumed a dominant position on American movie screens.

The war was nearly over when the German chief of staff, General Erich Ludendorff, asked the Imperial Ministry of War in Berlin to beef up its efforts to use motion pictures as a political weapon. "The war has demonstrated the superiority of the photograph and the film as a means of information and persuasion," he said. "Unfortunately our enemies have used their advantage over us in this field so thoroughly that they have inflicted a great deal of damage."[49] Belatedly, Ludendorff's appeal led to the formation of a Photo and Film Office in the German army and, only a few months before the war ended, to the construction of the massive studio complex of UFA, the *Universum Film Aktiengesellschaft,* a facility that was ready and waiting for a different war less than two decades later.

Although it is questionable whether film propaganda actually played as decisive a role in shaping American public opinion as Ludendorff suggests, the German and Allied officials films did provide a firsthand demonstration of the many ways motion pictures could be used to persuade and inform. Later, when the United States government began to produce its own films through the Army Signal Corps and the Committee on Public Information, it adopted many of the production techniques, advertising plans and exhibition patterns that were developed during the neutrality years by the European powers. Furthermore, official war newsreels were not the only form of motion picture propaganda released in the United States during the two and one-half years of American neutrality. American military leaders and government officials showed as much, or even more, interest in films which dealt directly with the United States' own preparation, or lack of preparation, for war.

**The Preparedness Films**

The public debate over American military preparedness began in the early months of the war. While the vast majority of the American people undoubtedly supported the president's neutrality policy, there was a sharp division of opinion regarding the best means of maintaining that neutral stance. Eventually this debate spilled over into a number of movies about preparedness.

On one side of the preparedness question were the pacifists led by Secretary of State Bryan and Senator Robert M. LaFollette. They argued that an aggressive American peace campaign was the surest way of keeping the country neutral and bringing the war to a speedy conclusion. This viewpoint was opposed by a group of Americans who felt that the European conflict demonstrated the country's need to improve its defenses. Under the leadership of Theodore Roosevelt, former Chief of Staff Leonard Wood, Representative Augustus P. Gardener, and Secretary of War Lindsay Garrison, the preparedness movement generated a stream of proposals designed to strengthen the nation's military readiness.[50]

As the war in Europe continued, the preparedness advocates began to organize their efforts to mobilize public opinion. In December 1914 the National Security League was formed at a meeting of one hundred and fifty public leaders in New York City. Together with the Army League and the

Navy League, the traditional champions of a strong military, the National Security League spearheaded the drive for American military preparedness.[51]

The preparedness controversy was one of the central issues facing the country during the neutrality years and it is hardly surprising that commercial film companies made an effort to exploit the public's interest in the subject. In January of 1915, the Lubin Company told the trade press that it had presented Secretary Daniels with a series of motion pictures showing Navy maneuvers and torpedo practice. Later in the year the Lubin Company also released two theatrical films which dealt with the European conflict: *The Rights of Man* and *The Nation's Peril*, a film which showed how the invention of a flying torpedo helped to foil an enemy attack on the United States.[52]

The Edison Company also released a preparedness film entitled *Manufacturing Big Guns for the Nation's Defense*. Advertising for the film stressed the fact that the film had been produced with the cooperation of the War Department, a statement which simply meant that Edison had to have the War Department's permission to shoot film in an armaments factory.[53]

During the submarine crisis in 1915, film companies stepped up efforts to link their preparedness films to military leaders and government officials. President Wilson was invited to a special screening of *Uncle Sam's Navy on Review* with the now familiar assurance that his attendance would not be used for advertising purposes.[54] Several months later the Eiko Film Company held up the release of its preparedness film, *Guarding Old Glory*, until it could secure endorsements from a number of military men. Eiko's general manager also wrote the president, trying to convince him that *Guarding Old Glory* was a film he could not afford to miss:

> It is strictly educational and free from all play features. The picture has been designed to stir up patriotism, and help recruiting. It has taken several months to make and seems to have been finished at the psychological [ly most effective] moment. We have shown the picture to Secretary of War Garrison, Secretary of the Navy Daniels, General Hugh Scott, General Leonard Wood, and Admiral Benson, each of whom has pronounced the picture to be most wonderful, very instructive, and [said it] will do a lot of good for the country.[55]

In many respects the summer of 1915 did seem to be "the psychological moment" to release a preparedness film. The sinking of the *Lusitania* had created a new surge of interest in preparedness and the membership in the various preparedness organizations increased dramatically. In June, the National Security League organized a Conference Committee on National Preparedness to coordinate the work of the many different organizations involved in the preparedness crusade. These organizations released a flood of pro-preparedness propaganda, and with increasing regularity, the preparedness organizations began to sponsor or produce moton pictures that advanced their cause.[56]

In September 1915, J. Stuart Blackton of the Vitagraph Company released *The Battle Cry of Peace,* a film that was probably the single most important preparedness film shown in the United States during the neutrality years. The film was based on *Defenseless America,* a book by the inventor and munitions manufacturer, Hudson Maxim. *Defenseless America* stressed the need to equip the U.S. military with modern weapons. In graphic terms, it also depicted the terrible fate awaiting an America betrayed from within by what Maxim referred to as "the dubs of peace."[57]

After discussing the project with Theodore Roosevelt, one of his neighbors at Oyster Bay, Blackton began production on *The Battle Cry of Peace* using extras from the Grand Army of the Republic and the National Guard to help him stage the film's spectacular battle sequences. Blackton's film told the story of a young American, John Harrison, who hears a lecture by Hudson Maxim (who plays himself) and is converted to the cause of preparedness. Harrison tries unsuccessfully to persuade his fiancee's father, Mr. Vandergriff, to abandon the Peace Movement, which has been infiltrated by enemy agents, and is unwittingly helping to stall a military appropriations bill in Congress. At a huge peace rally, Vandergriff releases a flock of doves just as an enemy shell comes crashing through the building. An unidentified, but vaguely German-looking, foreign power has begun its invasion of the United States. Armed with vastly superior weapons, they quickly reduce New York, and later Washington, to flaming rubble. Enemy soldiers shoot both Vandergriff and Harrison, whose fiancee is killed by her own mother to keep her from falling into the hands of the rapacious invaders.[58]

To help build public interest in the film Blackton staged a number of "invitation-only" screenings in New York and Washington prior to the film's general release. Each of these screenings gave Blackton the opportunity to pack the audience with government officials, military men and popular entertainers who were invariably linked to the film in the newspaper accounts which followed. Blackton secured official sponsorship for the film from the National Security League, the Army League, the American Red Cross and the American Legion.[59]

Blackton's representatives also invited President Wilson to one of the special screenings and although there is no record of the president's response, Blackton was able to obtain endorsements from a number of prominent figures including Secretary Garrison, General Leonard Wood, and Admiral George Dewey, all of whom appeared on screen at the end of the film, praising *The Battle Cry of Peace* with the aid of title cards.[60]

By the time the film premiered in New York in September 1915, Blackton had built enough momentum to turn the evening into a gigantic preparedness rally. In a theater draped with flags and bunting, Captain Jack Crawford, an actor in the film, began the evening's activities by attacking the pacifistic war

Figures 7 and 8.  German-looking soldiers in two scenes from J. Stuart Blackton's Vitagraph production of *The Battle Cry of Peace.* (Post-Newsweek Television Stations, Inc. and Blackhawk Films)

song, "I Didn't Raise My Boy to Be a Soldier." The audience also heard speeches from Hudson Maxim and from Blackton himself, who read a letter of praise from Theodore Roosevelt. In an obvious reference to attacks on his British upbringing, Blackton also revealed that he had recently become an American citizen.[61]

The tremendous publicity created by the prerelease screenings, celebrity endorsements, and preparedness rallies helped to turn *The Battle Cry of Peace* into a huge success at the box office. When the film was released nationwide, many exhibitors repeated Blackton's exhibition pattern, filling their theaters with soldiers, sailors and spokesmen from local preparedness organizations.[62]

Car maker Henry Ford, a leading pacifist, was so angered by the film that he took out full-page advertisements in 250 newspapers, denouncing *The Battle Cry of Peace* as a thinly disguised attempt to bring the United States into the war, an act sure to benefit Hudson Maxim's munitions company. The Vitagraph Company sued Ford for libel, but by the time the suit was settled the United States had already entered the First World War.[63]

In the same month that Blackton's film was released throughout the country, Thomas Dixon developed a sudden interest in the subject of preparedness. He wrote the president about his new project—*The Fall of a Nation*—a preparedness film which he claimed would rally public opinion for Wilson's "brave and patriotic foreign policy." With his letter, Dixon enclosed a brief synopsis of the story and asked the president to make any suggestions he thought necessary to ensure the film's success.[64]

Dixon's *Fall of a Nation* bore a remarkable resemblance to Blackton's *The Battle Cry of Peace*. It told the story of an unnamed, but vaguely German, invasion force taking Long Island with little more than token resistance. This easy conquest is prepared from within by a combination of enemy agents and unwitting pacifists. As the country is being ground under the heels of the ruthless invaders, one of the pacifists, an obvious caricature of William Jennings Bryan, is shown peeling potatoes in the enemy mess hall. Eventually, a large force of American women come to the rescue, distracting the foreign troops while their sons and husbands stage a successful counterattack.[65]

The president's response to Dixon's scenario was swift and pointed:

> I must say to you that I am sorry after reading the synopsis of your new enterprise, because I think the thing a great mistake. There is no need to stir up the nation in favor of national defense. It is already soberly and earnestly aware of its possible perils and of its duty, and I should deeply regret seeing any sort of excitement stirred in so grave a matter.[66]

Despite the president's negative reaction, Dixon continued with his project. He arranged for a serialized version of *The Fall of a Nation* to appear in the Sunday editions of several leading newspapers. The film, however, was not

Figure 9.    Portrait of J. Stuart Blackton.
            (Post-Newsweek Television Stations, Inc. and Blackhawk
            Films)

completed until almost a year later and although it was fairly successful at the box office, its subject was almost commonplace by the time it was finally released.[67]

By 1916, in fact, preparedness had become a familiar theme in American motion pictures. Several companies released news-film compilations much like the "official" war films of the European nations: *America Preparing* (The Kemble Film Company), a ten-part series featuring views of United States military encampments and training activities, and a similar newsreel series, *Uncle Sam's Defenders* (Mutual).[68] Other companies released theatrical films which highlighted different aspects of the preparedness controversy. In *If My Country Should Call,* a pacifistic mother drugs her son to keep him from enlisting in the army. She is about to commit suicide when she awakens, relieved to discover that the entire affair had been a very bad dream.[69]

American military skirmishes with Mexico provided the backdrop for Universal's *Liberty* preparedness series and several films such as *The Secret of the Submarine* and *For Uncle Sam's Navy* capitalized on the public's interest in submarine warfare.[70] Even Pearl White, the popular star of the movie serials, joined the preparedness parade with a film entitled *Pearl of the Army.* The Pathe Company mounted a massive publicity campaign for the film, distributing large posters of Pearl White as the "American Joan of Arc," and conducting screenwriting lessons in the newspapers using *Pearl of the Army* as an example for the would-be screenwriter to follow.[71]

In the midst of President Wilson's own preparedness campaign in early 1916, several preparedness organizations expanded their efforts to employ motion pictures as a propaganda weapon. The American Defense Society, a group which splintered away from the National Security League, staged a preparedness rally around the screening of newsreels showing U. S. Marines in Haiti. The American Defense Society also produced its own preparedness film, *America Unprepared,* which used animated maps and motion pictures to show one hundred and sixteen places along the Atlantic Coast that were undefended and vulnerable to an enemy attack, an exercise which, had a different organization produced the film, might have been accused of helping an enemy.[72] In April of the same year, producer Lewis J. Selznick and actress Clara Kimball Young formed an organization of motion picture exhibitors called the Motion Picture National Defense League. They developed plans to publicize preparedness in movie theaters throughout the country and they tried, unsuccessfully, to persuade Wilson to serve as the honorary president of their new organization.[73]

Although the president had initially been reluctant to become personally involved with screen propaganda, he did cooperate in the making of several preparedness films in the spring of 1916. The first of these films was Laurence Rubel's *Uncle Sam Awake.* In May, Wilson instructed his secretary Tumulty to help Rubel secure approval from the War Department to make a film designed to stimulate recruiting and promote military preparedness. Wilson also granted Rubel permission to shoot film of his Decoration Day speech to be used in conjunction with *Uncle Sam Awake.*[74]

At almost the same time, Wilson and Tumulty began to hear of plans for a feature-length film on the subject of industrial preparedness. At the urging of Howard E. Coffin, the chairman of the Naval Consulting Board, and Navy Secretary Josephus Daniels, the president agreed to let another filmmaker, Rufus Steele, photograph his Decoration Day speech at Arlington. He also gave Steele permission to use an extract from a preparedness speech he had given earlier in the year at Cleveland. Eventually, this material was edited into *The Eagle's Wings*, a film which combined footage taken in munitions plants with staged material showing the efforts of foreign diplomats to influence preparedness legislation in Congress.[75]

On the surface, motion picture propaganda released in the United States during the neutrality years seems to mirror the country's transformation from a neutral nation to an active participant in World War I. It is questionable, however, if the on-screen transition from pacifism to militarism, from neutrality to a pro-Allies position is as smooth as many film historians suggest.[76] Many of the important pacifist films such as Ince's *Civilization*, Griffith's *Intolerance* and Herbert Brennon's *War Brides* were not even released until 1916. Furthermore, pro-German war films were being shown in the United States until shortly before the American declaration of war. In any event, it would be a mistake to conclude that propaganda films dominated American movie screens during the two and one-half years of neutrality. The vast majority of American films continued to do what they had always done— provide inexpensive entertainment. It is significant that none of the major movie stars like Charles Chaplin, Douglas Fairbanks, Mary Pickford or William Hart appeared in a war-related film during this period.

For our purposes, the effects of motion picture propaganda are less important than the fact that motion pictures were being used so consistently in a new role. The "official" European news films and the preparedness films demonstrated a variety of ways in which motion pictures could be used to mobilize public opinion. The persuasive films of the neutrality years also underscored a surprising revelation about screen propaganda: the films were probably no more important than the setting they were shown in. Packed with a large crowd, the movie theater was a propaganda weapon of considerable value, an ideal place for patriotic speechmaking, fundraising, song-singing and flag-waving. Later in the war, this concept found fruition in the Committee on Public Information's Division of Four-Minute Men, an organization of public speakers who delivered brief patriotic talks between reel changes in movie theaters throughout the United States.

Certainly, by the time the United States entered the First World War, the credibility of motion picture propaganda was fairly well established. American military men, in particular, showed interest in screen propaganda. Not only had they attended numerous film screenings during the neutrality years, but they had, on occasion, given strong endorsements to films supportive of greater American military readiness. Furthermore the kind of cooperation developed between the chief executive, the War Department, and the film studios in the production of films like *The Eagle's Wings,* and *Uncle Sam Awake* later proved invaluable to the motion picture effort of the Committee on Public Information. In fact, the two filmmakers responsible for those films, Rufus Steele and Laurence Rubel, both made significant contributions to the United States government's own World War I film program: Steele, as head of the CPI Film Division, and Rubel, as head of the CPI's Bureau of War Photographs. Despite the flurry of prewar film activity, there is no evidence that either the U. S. government or the military made any plans to use motion pictures in the event of American participation in the war. Perhaps the uncertainty of American involvement encouraged procrastination. That delay, however, was the source of considerable confusion when the United States finally entered the war. By that time, the question was not whether motion pictures could be used to persuade and inform, but who, in a field of anxious competitors, would be responsible for using them.

# 3

# Flourishes and False Starts

When George Creel described the formation of the Committee on Public Information's film division, he made it sound as if the CPI had begun its film program in the earliest days of the war:

> At the very outset the Committee on Public Information made the decision that the three great agencies of appeal in the fight for public opinion were: The Written Word, the Spoken Word, and the Motion Picture. Even as the speaking forces and the writers of the Nation were mobilized, so were steps taken in the very first days to utilize every resource of the camera.[1]

There is no question that the CPI was ultimately responsible for the United States government's large-scale attempt to use motion pictures as a medium for propaganda and persuasion. By the time the CPI had fully developed its film program, regular filmgoers in the U.S. (and in many foreign countries) often saw films which the CPI had produced or officially approved. But the CPI film effort did not begin as quickly or develop as smoothly as Creel suggests. The CPI's Division of Films was not even established until more than five months after the U.S. entered the war. Even then, another six months passed before the Division of Films began full-scale operations.

What caused this delay? Why, after government officials and military leaders had shown so much interest in propaganda films during the neutrality period, did it take so long for the United States government to create its own film program?

In order to answer this question it is necessary to examine a confusing array of overlapping and occasionally conflicting efforts to use motion pictures as a propaganda weapon. The private film industry and its trade associations, the United States Army Signal Corps, and a number of service organizations such as the Red Cross and Y.M.C.A. each had an impact on the government's wartime film program. It is also important to understand something of the structure and objectives of the organization responsible for sorting out and coordinating these different film efforts—the United States government's official wartime propaganda agency—the Committee on Public Information.

## The World's Greatest Adventure in Advertising

On April 13, 1917, one week after American entry into the First World War, President Woodrow Wilson received a letter from the secretaries of state, war, and the Navy, asking him to establish a Committee on Public Information. The primary purpose of this committee would be to combine the functions of "censorship and publicity" within a single government agency. While stressing the importance of censorship to "safeguard all information of value to an enemy," the secretaries expressed their belief that the country's greatest needs were "confidence, enthusiasm, and service." To facilitate this effort, they suggested that "The chairman should be a civilian, preferably some writer of proven courage . . . able to gain the understanding and cooperation of the press and at the same time, rally the authors of the country to a work of service."[2]

The next day, Wilson instituted this recommendation through Executive Order 2594 (dated April 13, 1917), which created the Committee on Public Information. George Creel, a journalist with a long record of support for Wilson and his policies, was appointed as civilian chairman. Secretaries Lansing, Baker, and Daniels made up the rest of the committee.

Under Creel's dynamic leadership, the Committee on Public Information (CPI) greatly expanded previous government efforts in the fields of propaganda and public relations. It was Creel's firm belief that the CPI was not primarily a censorship agency. He felt its basic goals were to unify the country, to explain government war programs, and to build morale, a task Creel later described as "a plain publicity proposition, a vast enterprise in salesmanship, the world's greatest adventure in advertising."[3] Indeed, by the end of the war the CPI was capable of mounting a persuasive campaign that would be the envy of almost any modern advertising agency or public relations firm. CPI publicists could deliver a message to the American public through virtually every existing communication channel, including posters, photographs, press releases, billboards, newspapers, cartoons, public speeches, pamphlets, books, war exhibitions, and motion pictures.

Creel had expressed his preference for publicity over censorship some months before his appointment as chairman of the CPI. In early March 1917, he sent a brief to both Wilson and Daniels in which he outlined a plan for "voluntary censorship," and stressed the need for "expression rather than suppression."[4] At that time, however, the need for censorship seemed far more pressing than the need for publicity. Germany's resumption of unrestricted submarine warfare, and the subsequent break in German-American relations, brought the country nearer to war, and the need to restrict certain types of information, particularly in regard to ship movements, was self-evident.

In his official capacity as secretary of the Navy, Josephus Daniels had already begun to develop censorship plans. On March 17, 1917, he met with members of the press associations where he heard a variety of complaints about the dangers of heavy-handed military censorship. A former journalist himself, Daniels proposed a more benign voluntary censorship agreement with the press, assuring the newsmen that the government would "give them freely the information that would let them know what was going on."[5]

Although the need to control certain types of information provided much of the impetus for creating the CPI, there is little doubt that both Wilson and Daniels were well aware of Creel's ample skills as a publicist. As a journalist for the *Kansas City Independent,* the *Denver Post,* and the *Rocky Mountain News,* Creel had championed a number of progressive causes. His support of child labor legislation, laws to protect labor, municipal ownership, and election reform had earned him a justifiable reputation as a crusader, and had frequently embroiled him in controversy. Creel had become an early Wilson admirer and during the 1916 election campaign, he had worked in the publicity department of the Democratic National Committee, where he wrote press releases and organized a group of writers and publicists in support of the Democratic cause.[6]

During the campaign Creel also wrote a book, *Wilson and the Issues,* which defended the president's Mexican policy and his response to the *Lusitania* crisis; it also praised Josephus Daniels, whom Creel described as "the most maligned and misunderstood man in the United States today."[7] Creel's loyalty to Wilson and his administration was unquestioned, and he was evidently the only person considered for the chairmanship of the Committee on Public Information.

In April and May, as Creel began to gather his staff and build his organization, it is doubtful if anyone, Creel included, could have envisioned how wide-ranging the Committee's activities would become. As the CPI began to take shape it became apparent that domestic propaganda and foreign propaganda were sufficiently different to divide the CPI into two basic sections: Foreign and Domestic. The Foreign Section contained three subdivisions: the Foreign Press Bureau, the Wireless and Cable Service, and the Foreign Film Service. The Domestic Section was far larger, and to some extent, defies description. New divisions were started, divided, or eliminated based on a moment's inspiration or the availability of funding.

The News Division was one of the first to be established and it was undoubtedly the Committee's most important. It served as the official press bureau for all war-related information released by any government agency, including the White House, the military, the War Trade Board, the Justice Department, the Labor Department, and the War Industries Board.

The Division of Civic and Educational Cooperation published a stream of literature explaining America's reasons for entering the war, the nature of the enemy, and educational materials of a historical nature. Under the leadership of Charles Dana Gibson, the Division of Pictorial Publicity was responsible for producing patriotic posters and paintings. Other divisions within the CPI's domestic section dealt with war photographs, business management, women's war work, public speakers, and work among the foreign born.[8]

Both the Division of Pictures and the Division of Films were officially established on September 25, 1917, through Executive Order No. 2708. In part, the tardiness in creating a film division can be explained by the haste with which the CPI was forced to build its organization in the early days of the war. Faced with the task of gathering a staff, setting objectives and devising a means of meeting those objectives, the CPI, not surprisingly, did not begin its activities with a fully developed organizational chart. New divisions were formed as the need arose, and the CPI was still adding new divisions until shortly before the armistice.

But even the natural confusion and uncertainty associated with the start-up of any new organization do not entirely explain the long delay in creating an effective government film program. For almost a full year after America entered the war, the CPI listened to a variety of schemes from individual filmmakers, film companies, service organizations, and military leaders concerning the best way for the government to use motion picture propaganda. Long before the Division of Films was created, the National Association of the Motion Picture Industry (NAMPI), the Army Signal Corps, the American Red Cross, the Y.M.C.A., and councils of defense in many states had initiated their own film programs. When Louis Mack, the Division of Film's first chairman, assumed command of his new post, his first task might have been trying to come up with a meaningful job description for his own job. In a field teeming with would-be participants, hyperactive agents and professional idea-men, Mack probably wondered if there was any room left for a government film program.

## Mobilization of the Film Industry

During the early months of American participation in World War I, motion picture theaters across the country were transformed into centers of patriotic activity. Theater owners unfurled the flag. Lobby posters by artists like James Montgomery Flagg and Charles Dana Gibson urged moviegoers to enlist in the Army and be more productive on the job. On the screen, specially prepared slides encouraged each viewer to conserve food and fuel and to dig deep for the newest Liberty Loan drive. Motion picture newsreels documented the heroic effort of the Allies in Europe or provided a glimpse of the United States Army as it mobilized for action. Feature films offered even more dramatic reasons for total commitment to the war effort. In some films the kaiser was portrayed as a madman, a devil in a spiked helmet who could crush the helpless people of Belgium under his iron heel without a moment's remorse. Other films showed lecherous German soldiers shooting innocent civilians, throwing babies out windows, and ravishing Red Cross nurses. Between reel changes at such films, motion picture audiences might hear a brief patriotic speech, and as they left the theater, they might find a recruiting sergeant willing to escort them to the nearest enlistment office.

Much of this activity began spontaneously after the American declaration of war. In fact, the sheer volume of motion picture propaganda schemes created a problem. If each individual theater chain, trade association, and production company developed its own publicity campaign, their effectiveness would diminish. Furthermore, the government had specific messages about enlistment, conservation and war bonds which it needed to communicate to the American people within a certain time frame. If such efforts were to be successful, some means had to be found to coordinate the film industry's resources with the needs of the government.

One of the first ideas for coordinating these film activities came from Carl Laemmle, the president of the Universal Film Manufacturing Company. In late April 1917, Laemmle sent a letter to President Wilson in which he offered to turn the "entire facilities" of his company over to the United States government. He also proposed a plan in which Universal would provide the "nucleus" for an industry-wide committee to help the government develop an effective motion picture campaign.[9]

There is no record of Wilson's response to this offer, but it is doubtful if a single film company could have united the different branches of the highly competitive film industry. That difficult task eventually fell to a man who had already been in training for the job—William Brady, the president of the National Association of the Motion Picture Industry (NAMPI).

At the urging of Robert Wooley, the publicity manager for the First Liberty Loan drive, Brady created a joint industry-government committee in the first weeks of May 1917.[10] This committee had one objective: to foster the sale of war bonds through a motion picture publicity campaign. As chairman of this war bond committee, Brady organized a highly successful promotional effort. The NAMPI pledged to raise one million dollars for the First Liberty Loan drive, and also financed and distributed 8,000 copies of a short trailer in which President Wilson made a personal appeal to movie audiences to subscribe to the loan. During the First Liberty Loan drive Brady's committee also distributed 30,000 movie slides featuring such slogans as "Stand by the Flag and Subscribe to the Liberty Loan."[11]

Even though the war bond committee made a significant contribution to the first loan drive, Brady was dissatisfied with its make-up. He wrote the White House, complaining about "unknown meddlers" who were "trying to hand out screen publicity for their own personal advantage." He also told the president that he, and other key industry leaders, had met several times in June with George Creel. Together, Brady explained, they had begun to formulate a new industry war committee composed of men so powerful that they could "in two weeks to a month place a message in every part of the civilized world...."[12]

Less than a week later Wilson accepted Brady's offer and asked him to officially form an industry committee to work with George Creel and the Committee on Public Information. The president's letter gives some indication that the film industry's frantic prewar public relations campaign had not fallen on deaf ears and it was widely published in the industry's trade papers:

> It is in my mind not only to bring the motion picture industry into fullest and most effective contact with the nation's needs, but to give some measure of official recognition to an increasingly important factor in the development of our national life. The film has come to rank as a very high medium for the dissemination of public intelligence, and since it speaks a universal language it lends itself importantly to the presentation of America's plans and purposes. . . .[13]

Within a matter of days, Brady announced the formation of the War Cooperation Committee of the Motion Picture Industry. D. W. Griffith was appointed chairman, but since he was in Europe directing a propaganda picture at the request of the French and British governments, Brady assumed most of the committee's administrative duties.[14]

Working closely with Creel, Brady set up subcommittees to work with various agencies including the War Department, the Department of the Interior, the Aircraft Division, the War Camp Motion Picture Committee, the Commercial Economy Board, the Shipping Board, the American Red Cross (both a men's and women's division), and the Council of National Defense. In organizing these committees, Brady astutely enlisted the services of film stars, writers, studio executives, film distributors, equipment manufacturers, film exhibitors, and motion picture advertisers from virtually every important company within the American film industry in 1917. As a result, Brady's War Cooperation Committee possessed every conceivable resource necessary for mounting a successful motion picture publicity campaign. Not only could his committee produce films, it also had the means to ensure their distribution and exhibition in every state in the country.[15]

One of Brady's first assignments was to help the government develop a foreign film service which could help "teach the lessons of democracy in Europe."[16] At the urging of both Creel and Wilson, Brady established a new committee for this purpose in the first weeks of October 1917—the American Cinema Commission. Jules Brulator from the Eastman Kodak Company was appointed chairman and he selected three men who were to have been sent overseas to spearhead the American film campaign abroad:   Francis J. Marion, the president of the Kalem Company, was chosen as cinema commissioner for Italy; Patrick A. Powers from Universal was scheduled to go to France; and Walter W. Irwin, the general manager of the Vitagraph Company, was picked to run the film effort in Russia.[17]

This entire plan disintegrated before it could be put into operation and illustrates the kinds of problems facing both Brady and the CPI as they tried to develop a coherent film program in the early days of the war. There were immediate complaints from within the film industry that the American Cinema Commission would help a few companies corner the foreign film market. Representatives from the Red Cross, Y.M.C.A. and the Commission on Training Camp Activities complained that the American Cinema Commission would overlap work that they had already begun.[18] Eventually, George Creel gave up in disgust. In December of 1917 he formed the CPI's own version of the American Cinema Commission—the Foreign Film Service. This new CPI division performed precisely the same functions as the proposed Brady committee, and used some of the same personnel: Jules Brulator was appointed as chairman of the Foreign Film Service, and Frank Marion later served as the CPI's film representative in Mexico and Spain.[19]

Despite this setback, Brady's War Cooperation Committee provided a crucial link between the government and the film industry. It was responsible for producing and distributing a series of short promotional films and slides about food conservation for both the Department of Agriculture and Herbert Hoover's United States Food Administration. Similar projects were developed for the Departments of War and Navy in an effort to stimulate recruiting and encourage physical fitness. Theater owners displayed government posters in their lobbies, and helped Dr. Harry A. Garfield, head of the United States Fuel Administration, design slides and trailers to promote fuel conservation. And even this work, which was done free of charge, paled beside the industry's contributions to the Treasury Department.

Working closely with Treasury Secretary William Gibbs McAdoo, his assistant Oscar Price, and the department's chief publicity man, Frank R. Wilson, the industry made an invaluable contribution to the government's war bond campaigns. During the Second Liberty Loan, the industry produced 70,000 promotional slides and a series of five short films dramatizing the need to support the loan. Secretary McAdoo appeared in a short trailer made for the Third Liberty Loan, and 17,000 copies of the film were distributed throughout the country, accompanied by an elaborate set of Liberty Loan lobby posters. During the Fourth Liberty Loan the industry spent $250,000 producing thirty-eight short dramatic films, each with a leading actor or actress.[20]

As far as the American public was concerned, however, the industry's most visible contribution to the war effort was not the work of committees, but the work of the movie stars. Charles Chaplin, Douglas Fairbanks, Mary Pickford, Sessue Hayakawa, Pauline Frederick, Theda Bara, William Hart, and many others proved to be some of the most effective bond salespeople that the country possessed. Throughout the war their familiar faces were the focal point of countless patriotic rallies and Red Cross benefits. Stars traveled coast to coast, gathering millions of dollars in Liberty Loan subscriptions. Many contributed well-publicized sums from their own well-publicized bankrolls. Their war work generated publicity in the nation's newspapers and magazines, and drew large crowds to many war rallies.[21]

A number of famous film stars volunteered their services for government promotional films. *The Great Liberty Bond Hold-up,* a film donated to the government by the Lasky Studios, was based on the familiar screen character associated with each star. This short trailer was built around a single set: a bank teller selling war bonds through a bank window. Cowboy star William Hart buys his war bonds after frightening the poor teller with a display of six-gun prowess. Mary Pickford goes to the teller's window and purchases her war bonds as shyly and self-consciously as "the girl next door." Exuding boundless energy, Douglas Fairbanks leaps over the top of the teller's cage, grabs his war bonds, and is on his way out the door before he remembers to pay for them.[22]

In a short film entitled *The Bond* (also known as *Some Bonds I Have Known*), Charlie Chaplin made his own unique contribution to the Liberty Loan campaign. Dressed in his familiar tramp costume, Charlie surveys the bonds of friendship, love, marriage, and duty. At the end of the film he reveals the most important bond of all—the Liberty Bond. He then gives the audience a graphic demonstration of the kind of impact they can expect from their war bond purchases. Armed with an over-sized mallet bearing the inscription "Liberty Bonds," he pounds the unsuspecting kaiser senseless, landing blow after blow on the point of his ornate spiked helmet.[23]

These short skits were anything but masterpieces of film art, but they did show that the movie stars—and by association the film industry—were willing to do their bit for the war effort. These short films also illustrated another point: the machinery of entertainment could be applied to other ends.

After the declaration of war on April 6, 1917, the American film industry produced a flood of blatant propaganda films. In many the war was reduced to old-fashioned melodrama. Movie audiences were introduced to a number of new screen villains: mothers who discouraged their sons from enlisting, well-meaning pacifists who aided the enemy cause, spies and saboteurs who plotted the destruction of American society from within, German soldiers who committed horrible atrocities in occupied countries. In the end, of course, these screen villains were vanquished by ordinary American citizens, or through the heroic military effort of the Allies or the U.S. Expeditionary Forces.

To some extent, this kind of propaganda seems to exemplify George Creel's perception of "undesirable propaganda," materials which dealt excessively with the enemy or with the negative aspects of the war. In this respect, it is important to note that almost all of the government-produced CPI films were newsreels (or newsreel compilations), films which concentrated on glorifying America and documenting the mobilization of U.S. military forces. Hollywood filmmakers did this too, but they seemed more interested in the dramatic possibilities presented by the war. Although Creel and the CPI were embarrassed at times by the movie men's on-screen excesses, there was really no way of prohibiting films which so obviously did not give aid to the enemy.[24]

Several patriotic feature films had been released in the United States before the United States entered the war, and others were already in production when the war began. *On Dangerous Ground* was produced by William Brady's World Film Corporation in January of 1917 and is distinguished by the fact that it portrays a German officer in a somewhat favorable fashion. While visiting Germany, a young American doctor falls in love with a beautiful French spy. The war in Europe begins, and German soldiers capture the girl. Because the American doctor had earlier saved his life, a German officer helps the couple escape from Germany.[25]

In March of 1917, J. Stuart Blackton released *Womanhood, the Glory of the Nation*. After several unsuccessful attempts to persuade President Wilson to see the film, Blackton was able to line up endorsements from a number of defense societies and from several prominent government officials as well.[26] Another propaganda film in the prewar period was Pathe's *Mothers of France,* which starred the aging actress Sarah Bernhardt. The French government was partial owner of this film which *Moving Picture World*'s reviewer described as "propaganda so subtle and powerful that it must move even the most calloused and neutral observer."[27]

After America entered the war, a number of familiar themes began to emerge in the war films. The role of patriotic women was shown in films such as *Miss U.S.A.* (Fox, 1918), *A Daughter of France* (Fox, 1918), *Miss Jackie of the Army* (Mutual, 1917), *Joan of Plattsburg* (Goldwyn, 1918), and *A Little Patriot* (Pathe, 1918). Perhaps the most famous of these films was *The Little American* (Paramount-Artcraft, 1917), which was directed by Cecil B.

DeMille and starred Mary Pickford. *The Little American* told the complicated story of a young girl who goes to Europe to visit her sick aunt in France. On the way her ship, the *Veritania,* is sunk by a German submarine. After arriving in France, she meets a German-American diplomat she had known before the war. After witnessing numerous German atrocities in occupied France she says: "I stopped being neutral and became a human being." Although the German diplomat protects her for a time, she begins providing information about German gun placements to the French. Eventually, she is arrested, but just before she is to face the firing squad, she is rescued by the French military and sent home to the United States.[28]

Women were not always portrayed in such a positive light. In *The Man Who Was Afraid* a young man refuses to enlist because his mother would oppose it. Later, his patriotic friends taunt him by placing a doll outside with a sign attached calling him a coward. As he watches a passing military parade outside his window, he turns on his mother exclaiming, "My God, you made me a coward." Soon she relents and he goes on to become a war hero.[29]

Well-meaning mothers were not the only reason that young men failed to heed the call of duty in the movies, but films like *The Slacker* (Metro, 1917) and *Her Boy* (Metro, 1918) heaped ridicule on any "slacker" who refused to enlist in the military, regardless of his reason for refusing to serve. This point is driven home graphically in *The Kingdom of Hope,* a film in which a particularly patriotic mother dresses her children as soldiers and Red Cross nurses. At a meeting where a group of hand-wringing pacifists are drafting a peace resolution to send to the president, her children burst through the door chanting "War,War, We Want War," an act which shames the adults into abandoning their pacifistic ways.[30]

Other war films focused on a different side of the conflict at home. The evil machinations of German spies were revealed in films such as *The Secret Game* (Paramount, 1918). *The Eagle's Wings* (Wharton Prod. Company, 1918), *An Alien Enemy* (Paralta, 1918), and *The Hun Within* (Paramount, 1918). *The Prussian Cur,* a film directed by Raoul Walsh, advocated mob violence to deal with spies. It tells the story of a German agent who tries to induce an American worker into sabotaging an aircraft factory. The American reports the spy to the authorities. A group of German sympathizers tries to rescue the spy from jail, but at the last moment the Ku Klux Klan, riding furiously on horseback, arrives in town. They put the agent back in jail and force the sympathizers to kiss the American flag.[31]

Spies were not always treated so seriously. In many films they provided the perfect foil for screen comedy. *Swat the Spy* (Fox, 1918) showed the disloyal activities of a German butler and maid. Two little girls throw a pie at the servants' much-revered painting of the kaiser and subject the servant spy ring to a series of humorous humiliations.[32] *Spying the Spy* (Ebony, 1918) features the work of an inept spy catcher, who, after tracking down a German spy named Schwartz, throws a sack over his head and carts him off to the nearest police station. Schwartz, however, turns out to be a "respectable colored gentleman," and the would-be spy catcher is run out of the police station to begin his activities anew.[33]

Charlie Chaplin's war comedy—*Shoulder Arms*—was not released until near the Armistice in 1918. Chaplin plays an army private who captures the kaiser and brings him back through the enemy lines. He is about to be decorated for his bravery when he wakes up and discovers that his heroism has been a dream.[34] Many war-related screen comedies featured work behind the German lines. In *Doin' His Bit*, cartoon character Happy Hooligan steals the German war plans, and as he tries to make his escape he is forced to hide inside a large German gun. When the Germans fire the gun, they unwittingly send Happy Hooligan flying across no-man's land clinging perilously to the shell with the German war plans tucked securely in his pocket.[35] Mack Sennett's *Yankee Doodle in Berlin* was not released until 1919, but it treated the German high command with all the reverence of the Keystone Kops. Comedian Ben Turpin plays a German squad leader whose uncoordinated troops are a danger to everyone around them. They cannot march without running into each other and accidentally firing their guns. The crown prince decorates these men for heroically storming and capturing "a convent in Belgium." In the midst of this mayhem, an American spy masquerading as a woman wins the kaiser's affection and steals the German war plans. He (she) then crawls out on the balcony of the kaiser's mansion and relays these war plans through a series of hand-signals to his accomplice, a wireless operator who is camouflaged as a scarecrow in the kaiser's garden.[36]

In most of the industry's war films, the conflict was not treated as lightly or as absurdly. Many films reveled in the glories of the battlefield, showing Allied and American soldiers as they upheld the principles of democracy and freedom against a totalitarian enemy so vicious that women and children were in constant danger. One film of this type was *My Four Years in Germany,* which was produced by Mark M. Dintefass for Warner Brothers in 1918. It was based on a memoir by the same name written by James W. Gerard, the former American ambassador to Germany. Gerard's name provided an aura of authority that is freely encouraged in the first reel of the film, when a title card tells the audience that what they are seeing is "Fact Not Fiction." The German high command is introduced through a series of superimpositions comparing each of them to an animal. The kaiser, a man who seems to have mental problems, is shown riding a hobbyhorse while he makes plans to begin the First World War. After the brutal conquest of Belgium, German troops are shown slaughtering innocent refugees and tormenting prisoners of war. Near the end of the film one of the German officials boasts that "America

Won't Fight," a title which dissolves into newsreel footage of President Wilson and marching American soldiers. Soon American troops are seen fighting their way across the European battlefields. As he bayonets another German soldier, a young American doughboy turns to his companions and says, "I promised Dad I'd get six."[37]

President Wilson disapproved of Gerard's film, but in many cities across the nation audiences thronged to the film.[38] Effigies of the kaiser were burned outside theaters, and on several occasions, police had to be called out to disperse mobs of angry spectators.[39]

*My Four Years in Germany* was only one of a number of viciously anti-German films exhibited in American movie theaters during the war. Titles such as *To Hell with the Kaiser* (Metro, 1918) and *The Claws of the Hun* (Paramount, 1918) give some indication of the treatment the kaiser and his army received in these films. Probably the most famous "hate" film of World War I was entitled *The Kaiser, the Beast of Berlin* (Universal-Jewell, 1918), a film directed by Rupert Julian from a screenplay by Elliot Clawson. It catalogued every conceivable German atrocity from the sinking of the *Lusitania* to the rape of Belgium. Advertisements and posters for the picture urged American film audiences to "Hiss the Kaiser" every time he appeared on the screen.[40]

Films like *The Kaiser, the Beast of Berlin* and *My Four Years in Germany* fostered a terrifying image of the German people and their culture. The common German soldier was either portrayed as a mindless automaton, or a helpless pawn in the hands of the high command. German officers, in contrast, were invariably brutal and inhuman. Such movies even spawned the archetypal German screen villain. Erich von Stroheim, the great American director of the twenties, began his career in World War I acting the part of the incredibly cruel German officer. His monocle, shaved head, sabre-scarred cheek, and perpetual sneer became the standard for this stereotype in American popular culture. In *The Unbeliever,* one of the last films made by the Edison Company, von Stroheim plays a German officer so nasty that he frightens his own men. In one scene, he murders an old woman and child, and then burns their house to the ground. In his lust for a young Belgian maid, he kills a woman who is trying to protect her. Eventually his own troops rebel against his beastly behavior and shoot him in the back.[41]

Von Stroheim repeated this role in the lavishly mounted Universal production of *Heart of Humanity*. In one of the more memorable scenes in the film, von Stroheim attacks a Red Cross nurse. Her crying baby distracts him, and in a fit of anger, he throws the child out of the bedroom window. He turns back to the distraught woman, sneers, and calmly begins to unbutton his tunic. The woman flees to another room, ready to kill herself rather than submit to him. At the last moment, her soldier husband, who is conveniently nearby, fights his way into the building and shoots the German officer in the heart.[42]

On at least one occasion, President Wilson and his wife actually helped to moderate the content of a war film. That film was *Hearts of the World*, a picture which D. W. Griffith had directed at the request of the French and British governments. Griffith himself was actually responsible for the Wilsons' involvement with the picture. In the spring of 1918, he wrote Wilson's secretary Tumulty trying to convince him that the president should see *Hearts of the World*. "It has been hailed," Griffith bragged, "as the biggest propaganda to stir up patriotism yet put forth."[43]

There is no record of Wilson's response to this invitation, but several months later, Tumulty heard again from one of Griffith's representatives who told of the "keen interest" the British government had shown in the film, and who claimed that "Mr. Lloyd George himself had actually participated in the work."[44] Eventually, Wilson and his wife agreed to attend the film's Washington premiere in early June 1918. This presidential screening, however, did not produce the results Griffith expected. After seeing the film, Mrs. Wilson sent a wire to Griffith which caused him to spend "a sleepless night and a troubled day" trying to sort out her criticism of the film.[45] Griffith's lengthy response to Mrs. Wilson reveals not only his views about film propaganda, but his motivation for making *Hearts of the World*:

> When we deal with the general public as a whole, we deal with a very very stolid hard animal to move or impress. We must hit hard to touch them. In trying to bring home the truth of what they have suffered over there in an intimate human way, so that people so far away from the struggle could understand and want to strain every nerve to help them, I fell into the error which you so generously reminded me of, and overshot the mark. . . .
>
> I think that by eliminating the two powerful acting scenes, particularly where the Germans are concerned, and leaving more to the imagination, we will have a play that will not only hit the masses but not offend the refined and sensitive spirits such as yourself; otherwise, I shall, indeed, be a very disappointed, broken individual, for my hopes and work and prayers have been so bound up in this, that unless it is pleasing in your household, I feel that everything has been in vain. . . .[46]

Griffith arranged for one of his representatives to meet personally with Mrs. Wilson to discuss possible changes, and the president, too, expressed a willingness to help. As a result of their suggestions, Griffith evidently eliminated several sequences from the film and entirely reshot a scene in which actress Lillian Gish is brutally whipped by a German soldier.[47]

Such attempts to tone down war films were rare during the Great War, but it is important to remember that the vast majority of Hollywood films

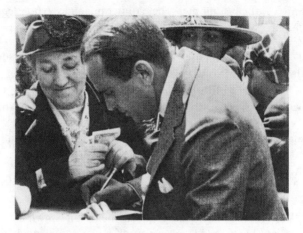

Figure 10.   Douglas Fairbanks signs up fan for the Liberty Loan.
(Post Newsweek Television Stations, Inc. and
Blackhawk Films)

were not built around images of an insane kaiser or German atrocities. In many films the war was nothing more than a convenient backdrop or setting. Most films ignored the war entirely, providing American audiences with comedies, romances and adventures that may have helped them forget the war. Some film companies purposely avoided war-related subjects out of the belief that film viewers had enough on their minds without being reminded of battlefield horrors and the dangers facing their friends and loved ones in the service. There was even a fear in some quarters that excessive screen violence might actually undermine the war effort by discouraging enlistment.[48]

While the film industry undoubtedly felt that its theatrical propaganda films were making a significant contribution to the government's war effort, neither the government nor the CPI had asked for them. In part, the flood of wartime film activity can be explained by the natural desire to help one's country in a time of crisis. Like many groups in American society, the men and women of the American film industry were anxious to "do their bit." It is also possible that propaganda films were good business: equating movie-going with patriotism may have encouraged attendance. Another reason may have been the industry's prewar public relations campaign which stressed the power of the motion picture to "educate and inform" as well as entertain.

Certainly, the United States government did not have to draft the American film industry. Initially, at least, the industry's War Cooperation Committee seemed the perfect tool for building a joint government-industry film effort. With so many willing and experienced volunteers, the need for a government film division within the CPI did not seem so pressing.

Figure 11. The industry's War Cooperation Committee poses for a photograph in Washington. (War Department Photo, National Archives)

Figure 12.  Charlie Chaplin directs the band at a huge Washington
Liberty Loan rally.
(Post-Newsweek Television Stations, Inc. and
Blackhawk Films)

Figure 13.  Mary Pickford in *The Great Liberty Bond Hold-up*.
(Post-Newsweek Television Stations, Inc. and
Blackhawk Films)

Figure 14. Actress Pauline Frederick wearing a Liberty Bond crown in "Stake Uncle Sam to Play Your Hand," an industry-sponsored Liberty Loan film. (War Department Photo, National Archives)

Figure 15.   The Germans execute nurse Edith Cavell in Select
Picture Corporation's 1918 film, *The Cavell Case*.
(War Department Photo, National Archives)

Figures 16 and 17. Before and after: The "slacker" son goes off to war in *The Man Who Was Afraid*.
(Post-Newsweek Television Stations, Inc. and Blackhawk Films)

Figure 18.  Patriotic children interrupt the pacifists' rally with some marching and flag-waving in *The Kingdom of Hope.* (Post-Newsweek Television Stations. Inc. and Blackhawk Films)

Figure 19. *The Eagle's Wings*: German saboteur captured by the Secret Service as he puts explosives in lumps of coal. (War Department Photo, National Archives)

Figure 20.  German butler and wife toast the kaiser's portrait in
*Swat the Spy.*
(Post-Newsweek Television Stations, Inc. and
Blackhawk Films)

Figure 21.  A twist on the pie-in-the-face in *Swat the Spy.*
(Post-Newsweek Television Stations, Inc. and
Blackhawk Films)

Figures 22 and 23. The war in slapstick—"heroic" German soldiers and cut-rate medals—in Mack Sennett's *Yankee Doodle in Berlin.*
(Post-Newsweek Television Stations, Inc. and Blackhawk Films).

Figure 24.  The title for *My Fours Years in Germany* highlighted
Gerard's participation.
(Post-Newsweek Television Stations, Inc. and Blackhawk
Films)

Figure 25.  Actor portraying Ambassador Gerard, center frame,
repudiates Germans' statement that America won't fight.
(Post-Newsweek Television Stations, Inc. and Blackhawk
Films)

Figure 26. The kaiser wads up the American flag in a scene from *To Hell with the Kaiser*. (War Department Photo, National Archives)

Figure 27.   A very literal representation from *To Hell with the Kaiser*.
(War Department Photo, National Archives)

Figure 28. The kaiser's War Council in *The Kaiser, the Beast of Berlin.* (War Department Photo, National Archives)

Figure 29.  The brutal German occupation of Belgium in *The Kaiser, the Beast of Berlin*. (War Department Photo. National Archives)

Figure 30.   Erich von Stroheim as the cruel German officer in *The
            Unbeliever*.
            (Post-Newsweek Television Stations, Inc. and Blackhawk
            Films)

Figure 31.   *Heart of Humanity*: As starving Belgians watch, the
            Germans dump milk donated by the American Red
            Cross.
            (Post-Newsweek Television Stations, Inc. and Blackhawk
            Films)

Figure 32.   Von Stroheim sends his men away so he can be alone with the nurse (Dorothy Phillips) in *Heart of Humanity*. (Post-Newsweek Television Stations, Inc. and Blackhawk Films)

Figure 33.   A crying baby, just before it is thrown out the window in *Heart of Humanity*. (Post-Newsweek Television Stations, Inc. and Blackhawk Films)

Figure 34.   Contemporary newsreel footage showing D. W. Griffith, left of camera, in the trenches in Europe. (Post-Newsweek Television Stations, Inc. and Blackhawk Films)

**The Signal Corps Goes into Production**

On July 21, 1917, the secretary of war designated the U.S. Army Signal Corps as the agency responsible for providing the still photographs and motion pictures for a "Pictorial History of the War of 1917."[49] This was an entirely new assignment for the Signal Corps and ultimately provided the foundation for the CPI's World War I film program. From its inception, the Signal Corps' primary responsibility had been military communications. Although still photographers had been at work in the military since the Civil War, the Signal Corps' experience with motion picture photography was extremely limited. When the war began, photography was basically viewed as an aid to reconnaissance and artillery spotting. Aerial photography in particular seemed to offer the most direct military applications. Pictures taken from a plane or balloon could be used to build up detailed battlefield mosaic maps, and until May 1918, the fledgling Army Air Service was actually located within the Signal Corps.[50]

The Signal Corps' records provide little insight into the motivation behind this new assignment. The *New York Times* described the Signal Corps' mission to produce a filmed history of the war as "following in the example of France and Great Britain,"[51] an explanation which seems plausible given the great interest American military leaders had shown in the so-called "official films" of the neutrality years. Another reason may have been the military's desire to use films for training purposes, an undertaking which clearly favored the development of film units within the military. While civilian newsreel cameramen might have been willing to shoot films for the military, they would also have presented a security risk. Furthermore, a film crew working under direct military control was probably more capable of providing material which could be used for training purposes.

Like most branches of the American military, the Signal Corps was woefully unprepared when the First World War began. Due to a lack of trained personnel, equipment and supplies, the development of the Signal Corps' Photographic Section was a slow and painful process. The additional burden of producing a visual history of the war simply added to these problems. In the beginning, it is doubtful if the Signal Corps fully appreciated the enormity of such an undertaking. Shooting a motion picture history of the First World War would have taxed the resources of the largest Hollywood film companies. It is not surprising, then, that it took almost a full year before the Signal Corps began producing films on a regular basis.

The Signal Corps had sent one of its photographic officers, Lieutenant Paul Miller, to France before the secretary of war gave the Corps its new film history assignment. Miller had accompanied General Pershing and his staff on their first visit to France in late May 1917, a mission designed to bolster

Allied morale and to help the General Staff make plans for the arrival of American troops. At that time Miller began a study of the methods and equipment used in the photographic departments of the Allied armies. After surveying the situation, Miller concluded that the Signal Corps would have to ship most of its film stock and cameras from the United States. To provide a secure means of processing film in France, he also rented a film laboratory for the Signal Corps at St. Quen in Paris.[52]

The St. Quen laboratory turned out to be a terrible mistake. It had been the Eclair Company's newsreel lab prior to the war, but by the time the Signal Corps obtained it, it had been out of operation for two years. The Corps worked feverishly trying to get the laboratory back into working order, but in the winter of 1917 the furnace went down and the temperature in the building could not be raised over fifty degrees Fahrenheit. It was impossible to process film under such conditions and the Signal Corps was forced to sublet much of its processing work to the Pathe Company. Finally, in February 1918, the Signal Corps moved its entire photographic operations to the Pathe plant in Vincennes where they remained until the end of the war.[53]

From the beginning of the war the Signal Corps was plagued by organizational problems. Initially, the Corps planned to place a four-man photographic unit with each military division. Each unit was to contain one motion picture photographer, one still photographer, and two assistants. Additional units were to be assigned to the Sea Transport Service, Supply Service and service organizations like the Red Cross and Salvation Army. By the end of the war a total of thirty-eight photographic units had been put in the field, although a shortage of manpower usually reduced these units to a crew of three men.[54]

There is considerable confusion concerning the disposition of film shot by these Signal Corps photographic units. George Creel claimed that film shot by Signal Corps cinematographers in France was "delivered, undeveloped, to the Chief of Staff for transmission to the War College Division."[55] The Signal Corps' records, however, suggest a somewhat different pattern for the way this film was handled. After film was shot in the field, it was turned in to the Signal Corps laboratory for processing. There, under the direction of a press officer from the Intelligence Section, the film was censored and the descriptive titles accompanying the film were checked for accuracy. Then prints were made and duplicate negatives were shipped to the War College in Washington.[56] It is possible, of course, that the film was censored again in the U. S. before it was turned over to the CPI, a procedure which would help to explain Creel's account. But having gone to the trouble of establishing its own film laboratory in France, the Signal Corps would be unlikely to ship undeveloped film back to the United States, particularly when the Corps needed to keep track of the work its photographers were doing in the field.

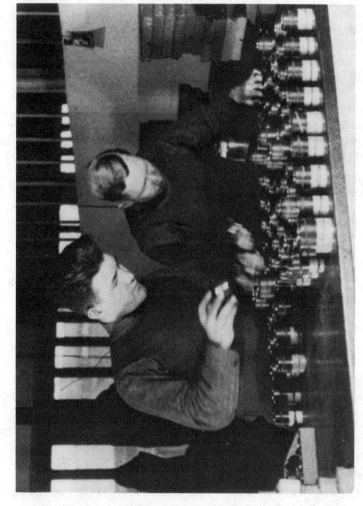

Figure 35.   Sorting film in the Signal Corps Photo Laboratory.
(Signal Corps Photo. National Archives)

One of the biggest problems facing the Signal Corps was an acute shortage of trained personnel. In August 1917, there were only twenty-five men in the Photographic Section, and cinematographers were in such short supply that only four motion picture cameramen were in the field as late as March 1918.[57]

In order to provide trained cameramen the Signal Corps established two training schools in the United States. A school of Land Photography was created at Columbia University on January 1, 1918, and six weeks later a school of Aerial Photography opened at the Eastman Kodak Company in Rochester, New York. By that time the Signal Corps had decided that land and aerial photography were so different in method and purpose that they should be separated. Later in the war all aerial photography was removed from the Signal Corps' jurisdiction and given to the new Army Air Service.[58]

Although a few Hollywood professionals served in the Signal Corps during the First World War, most of the men in these schools had no prior photographic experience.[59] The Signal Corps was able to obtain a few experienced men through direct commission or by transferring men who were already in other branches of the military service. Later in the war, as the CPI began to expand its own use of Signal Corps film material, the CPI helped the Signal Corps find experienced film personnel. None of this help really solved the Signal Corps' problems. The Corps' training schools (2,500 students at Rochester alone) did not begin graduating classes until June of 1918. As a result, few of these students ever reached France. Nevertheless, by the end of the war the total strength of the Photographic Section included ninety-two officers and four hundred and ninety-eight enlisted men. The vast majority of these men were actually employed in the Signal Corps laboratory, and there was a shortage of trained cameramen in the field until just shortly before the armistice was signed in November 1918.[60]

Even when the Signal Corps found a trained cinematographer, it had a difficult time providing him with a camera and film stock. The monthly reports of the Signal Corps Photographic Section contain a familiar litany: Send more men. Send more cameras. Send more film. On several occasions the Signal Corps was able to purchase film stock in France, but cameras were a different matter. As late as December 1917 the Corps possessed only five working cameras, and the first shipment of new cameras from the United States did not arrive in France until the end of January 1918.[61] At first the Signal Corps tried to solve this problem by buying old Pathe studio cameras in France, but these cameras were usually more of a hindrance than a help in the field. They were heavy, broke down frequently, and were equipped with an awkward exterior magazine. Motion picture cameramen in the Signal Corps Photographic Units tended to monopolize all the men of the unit just to help move equipment, a situation which prompted the chief signal officer to

Figure 36. Signal Corps cameraman in the trenches with a lightweight camera, precisely the kind the Signal Corps most needed.
(Signal Corps Photo, National Archives)

Figure 37. France, 1918: Signal Corps cameraman taking pictures from a wrecked building. (Signal Corps Photo, National Archives)

remind his crews that "it was the duty of the still photographer to make still photographs and not to act as assistant to the motion picture operator."[62]

What the Signal Corps cameramen needed in the field was a sturdy, lightweight newsreel camera. Although the Corps eventually developed a camera of this kind, during the first year of the war its cameramen were often forced to make do with equipment that was poorly suited for the job at hand.[63]

The difficulty of finding suitable camera lenses added to the Signal Corps' equipment problems. Prior to the war the Germans dominated the optical business and many months passed before American manufacturers began producing an adequate supply of lenses. Again, the Signal Corps tried to purchase a few lenses in France, but the demand for lenses in other military applications made it hard to buy an adequate quantity.[64]

The Signal Corps' assignment to produce a "pictorial history of the war" was another source of confusion in the early months of the war. Given the inexperience of its cameramen and the uncertainty surrounding its charge to shoot a historical record of the war, it is hardly surprising that coverage of many activities was fragmented and that the descriptive titles accompanying that film were often vague and misleading. In an effort to remedy this situation, Paul Miller suggested a new approach:

> In order to get historical and news events it is necessary to know in advance, movements of troops, manoeuvers, etc., in order to get a continuous and connected story of the progress of the American Army in France. It should be the duty of one officer to work in conjunction with the Intelligence Section, thus being able to keep the cameramen at work on a prearranged plan instead of getting disconnected bits of story from various sources.[65]

Eventually most of Miller's suggestions were adopted. An officer was assigned to each division to coordinate assignments with the Photographic Section. The key to this entire plan was an elaborate syllabus which the Signal Corps issued to its photographic units in March 1918. This syllabus gave the camera crews some sense of direction: when they were not shooting film of their own divisions, the syllabus outlined other material they should be gathering, i.e., documenting the work, equipment and facilities of the Quartermaster Corps, Red Cross or the Equipment Division.[66]

This syllabus also helps to explain something of the character of Signal Corps photography in the Great War. Film shot according to the syllabus was what the Signal Corps itself referred to as "record photography," motion pictures which simply documented buildings, equipment or procedures. Most of this footage was static and could have been shot as easily, and probably as well, with a still camera. Later in the war, when the CPI began using Signal Corps motion pictures in its own propaganda work, the Corps recognized the difference between shooting record films and films of "non-recurrent events."

Figure 38. Signal Corps cameraman, center, photographing military bombardment in France. (Signal Corps Photo, National Archives)

When shooting film for use in the CPI productions, Signal Corps cinematographers were encouraged to shoot from "some unusual viewpoint . . . to suggest local color or with something of local interest in the foreground."[67]

The Signal Corps collection in the National Archive reveals that the vast majority of its films fit into the category of "record photography." Action footage, much less battlefield footage, is rare, and most films concentrate on scenes behind the lines: parades, inspections, equipment demonstrations, buildings and procedures.

It took a little more than a year for the Signal Corps to sort out what was needed to produce a film history of the war. By that time the Corps had built an organization with trained personnel, adequate equipment, and a working laboratory. The vast majority of Signal Corps films were actually shot in the closing days of the war and this growth can be graphically demonstrated by laboratory records which show how much film the Signal Corps laboratory processed in each month of the war:

| | | |
|---|---|---|
| December | 1917 | 2,500 feet of film |
| January | 1918 | 5,000 feet of film |
| February | 1918 | 10,000 feet of film |
| March | 1918 | 24,000 feet of film |
| April | 1918 | 10,000 feet of film |
| May | 1918 | 35,000 feet of film |
| June | 1918 | 30,000 feet of film |
| July | 1918 | 65,000 feet of film |
| August | 1918 | 53,000 feet of film |
| September | 1918 | 70,000 feet of film |
| October | 1918 | 82,000 feet of film |
| November | 1918 | 118,000 feet of film |
| December | 1918 | 70,000 feet of film[68] |

Compared to the work of World War II combat photographers, much of this footage is rather dull and uninspiring, but that does not diminish the Signal Corps' accomplishment. Despite the many problems the Signal Corps faced in developing an effective organization, its cameramen managed to shoot almost one million feet of film in Europe and in the United States. Considering the Corps' lack of previous filmmaking experience and its lack of preparedness when the war began, this was a remarkable achievement. The chief signal officer described this effort with understandable pride:

The obvious and important uses in the theater of war of military photography, important as they are, cannot overshadow the later purposes to be served by both motion pictures and still photographs taken during the war period. Such pictures furnish a record for the present and future generations such as never before was available. Soldiers will study them for technical instruction, while civilian students will be enabled to employ them as valuable and interesting aids to historical research.

The photograph preserves a faithful reproduction of events and thus gives to military history a quality of exactness that never before was able to be incorporated in it.

What would the world not give for similar moving pictures of Washington's army or Napoleon's campaigns?[69]

## The Formation of the Division of Films

The Signal Corps' surprising effort to provide a historical record of the First World War on film provided the impetus for creating the CPI's Division of Films. A short time after the Signal Corps was designated as the agency responsible for producing a film history of the war, it occurred to George Creel that the Signal Corps motion pictures had immense "publicity value." Creel went to Secretary of War Newton Baker and secured an agreement which made the CPI the sole distributing agency for all films and photographs taken by Signal Corps photographers, probably the single most important act in the development of the United States government's World War I film campaign. In order to handle this new assignment, the CPI's Division of Films and its Division of Pictures were established (by Executive Order 2708) on September 25, 1917.[70]

In the beginning, the work of these two divisions frequently overlapped. The Division of Pictures was primarily responsible for issuing permits to commercial photographers or newsreel cameramen who wanted to take pictures of military activities. This was an outgrowth of the CPI's "voluntary censorship" plan and started before the Division of Pictures and Division of Films were officially established. Photographers who wanted to shoot film at Army or Navy installations were required to submit an application to the Division of Pictures, which also controlled the release or publication of photographs taken under the permit system, making sure that military security was not compromised. All cameramen were required to deposit a print of their pictures or films with the CPI before their pictures could be released.[71]

The personnel in both divisions changed frequently during the first months of operation. Kendall J. Banning was the first director of the Division of Pictures, but he also handled most of the CPI's early motion picture activities, serving as a liaison between the CPI and the film industry's War Cooperation Committee. Within a month of his appointment to the Division of Pictures, Banning was commissioned as a Major in the Signal Corps reserve and transferred to Washington. As head of the Signal Corps News and Publicity Division, Banning was instrumental in helping both the Signal

Corps and the CPI obtain experienced cameramen and film editors. Later in the war, Banning served as Liaison Officer between the Signal Corps and the CPI, where he played a vital role in coordinating the joint film activities of both agencies.[72]

Laurence E. Rubel replaced Banning as director of the Division of Pictures in October 1917. Rubel, it will be recalled, had worked with the War Department during the neutrality years to produce the preparedness film *Uncle Sam Awakes*. Rubel continued to operate the CPI's permit system, but was also instrumental in helping Creel chart the course for the Division of Films.[73]

Many historical accounts point to Charles S. Hart as the director of the Division of Films.[74] Hart, however, did not take charge of the film division until sometime in March or April of 1918. For the first six months of the film division's existence, the director was Louis B. Mack, a Chicago lawyer with virtually no prior film experience.[75]

It is easy to understand Mack's omission from the historical record. Under his tenure as director of the Division of Films, there was little indication that motion pictures would play anything but a minor role in the CPI's propaganda effort. Initially, George Creel hoped that the CPI could rely on either private producers or the industry's War Cooperation Committee to produce any films that the government might need. Certainly, in the early stages of the war, the industry's patriotic fervor seemed to justify Creel's expectations. Significantly, one of Creel's first directives to Louis Mack emphasized the need to maintain the industry's goodwill: he instructed Mack to avoid any form of direct competition with the commercial film industry.[76]

The CPI's desire to minimize conflict with existing wartime film programs extended to the field of film exhibition, an area where both the American Red Cross, and the state councils of defense had established a foothold long before the Division of Films began operation. As a result, the CPI's early role was limited to providing Signal Corps films to the state councils or the Red Cross, who were actually responsible for exhibiting the films.[77] With the exception of a few special Red Cross benefit screenings, no admission was charged for films distributed in this manner, and most films were shown only to patriotic societies, schools and churches, a procedure which clearly echoed Creel's desire to avoid conflict with commercial film interests. According to Creel, the CPI distributed a number of Signal Corps films in this manner during the first six months of the war:

> *The 1917 Recruit* (training of the National Army)
> *The Second Liberty Loan*
> *Ready for the Fight* (Artillery and Cavalry maneuvers)
> *Soldiers of the Sea* (Marine Corps in training)

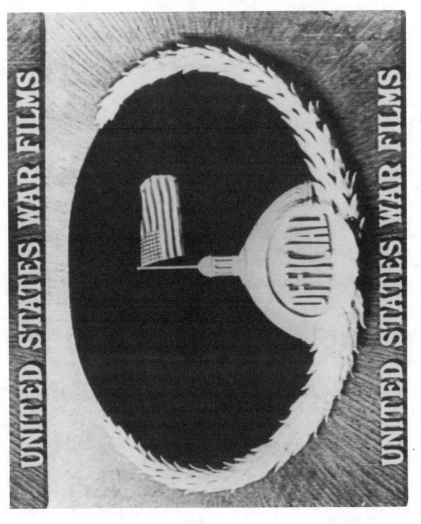

Figure 39. Animated title sequence from an early Signal Corps-CPI war film which was distributed by the Red Cross. (Post Newsweek Television Stations, Inc. and Blackhawk Films)

*Torpedo Boat Destroyers* (naval maneuvers)
*Submarines*
*Army and Navy Sports*
*The Spirit of 1917*
*In a Southern Camp* (general Army maneuvers)
*The Lumber Jack*
*The Medical Officer's Reserve Corps in Action*
*American Ambulances*
*Labor's Part in Democracy's War*
*Annapolis*
*Fire and Gas*[78]

Where did these films come from? As we have already seen, the Signal Corps was just beginning to shoot film by the end of 1917 and the Division of Films had not fully developed its own production unit. Some of these films may actually have been shot by commercial newsreel cameramen. Several newsreel companies had released patriotic newsreels in the United States even before the Division of Films was created, and they continued this kind of production, in a limited way, throughout the war.[79] Another possible source for these films may have been the CPI's "voluntary censorship" plan, which required cameramen to deposit a print of their film with the CPI's Divison of Pictures, a procedure which gave the CPI access to material which it could have edited into patriotic newsreels.

Regardless of who produced these pictures, the Division of Film's early film effort was clearly overshadowed by the work of the American Red Cross. During the neutrality period the Red Cross had sponsored a number of Allied film screenings, and it continued this lucrative fundraising activity long after American entry into the war. Encouraged by the success of these screenings, the Red Cross began to expand its own film production work under the auspices of the American Relief Clearing House in Paris. In July of 1917, cameraman Merl LaVoy returned from France with *Heroic France, the Allies in Action,* an eight-reel picture which showed scenes from the battlefield in France, as well as views of leading French and British officials.[80]

LaVoy's work was soon eclipsed by a steady stream of films produced by Paul D. Rainey, who, along with two cameramen, arrived at the American Relief Clearing House in Paris shortly after the American declaration of war. For a time, at least, Rainey's status with the Signal Corps and the American Expeditionary Forces was a source of considerable confusion. At some point in the summer of 1917, Rainey wrangled permission from General John Pershing to shoot film of the A.E.F. provided that he did not interrupt their work and that he submit his films to military censorship.[81]

Once in the field, however, Rainey completely ignored these restrictions. He began billing himself as "The Official Photographer of the United States Army."[82] While the Signal Corps was trying to sort out his actual position, Rainey shot films, processed them at the Red Cross laboratory in Paris, and shipped them to the United States where they were incorporated into Red Cross films. If there was footage left over, it was sold to commercial newsreel companies who were desperate for footage of the war. For a time, Rainey was probably shooting more film than the entire Signal Corps, and it was not until September of 1917 that the Army finally forced him to process his film at the Signal Corps' lab and to furnish a copy of his films for the Signal Corps archives.[83]

The work of men like LaVoy and Rainey enabled the Red Cross to establish a dominant position during the beginning stages of the war; the CPI tacitly acknowledged this situation in an agreement it worked out with the Red Cross in October 1917. Under the terms of this agreement, the Red Cross promised to sell the commercial newsreel companies a certain amount of footage each week, while retaining the right to use the material in their own lucrative benefit productions.[84]

By the time Louis Mack became chairman of the CPI's Division of Films, the Red Cross, the Signal Corps and the industry's War Cooperation Committee had already developed their own motion picture programs. Operating under Creel's directive to avoid conflict with existing film campaigns, Mack made only a limited attempt to expand the role played by the Division of Films. One tentative step in this direction occurred near the end of 1917 when Mack announced that the Division of Films was going to produce three feature-length government propaganda films: *The Immigrant,* a film to explain democratic principles to recent immigrants; *Columbia,* a film featuring patriotic events from American history; and *German Spies,* a film to provide information about spies operating on the home front. However, only one of these films, *The Immigrant,* was actually completed.[85]

Mack's other innovation, the creation of a Scenario Department within the Division of Films, was no more successful than his venture in feature filmmaking. To head this new department, Mack secured the services of Dr. George Pierce Baker from Harvard University. Baker assembled a staff of college professors and professional screenwriters who were supposed to work in an advisory capacity, checking the accuracy of historical information in government films and helping to gather information on current public opinion to guide the CPI's future film efforts. Mack hoped the Scenario Department could encourage commercial film producers to make films for the government, but there is no evidence that the Scenario Department succeeded in convincing anyone to do anything.[86] Creel, significantly, omits any mention of Mack's work in this area, and the CPI established an entirely new Scenario Department within the Division of Films in June 1918.

During Louis Mack's tenure as chairman of the Division of Films, the U.S. government's official World War I propaganda agency stayed very much on the fringe of the war-related film business. In this early period, the CPI's basic activity was issuing permits to commercial cameramen. Although Creel had secured distribution rights to all Signal Corps films, the Corps initially had trouble finding cameras and cameramen, much less making films. And when it did produce a film, the Division of Films simply funneled it through existing distribution channels already controlled by the councils of defense and American Red Cross. Even the development of the CPI's foreign film campaign was based on a previous program: the American Cinema Commission created by the film industry's War Cooperation Committee. It took six months for the CPI to create its Division of Films, and for the six months that Louis Mack served as chairman, there was almost no indication that the CPI's film effort would do anything more than supplement the work that others had begun.

# 4

# Reorganization and Expansion

In January 1918, George Creel received what he described as an "insulting" letter concerning the early CPI film effort.[1] It was written by William A. Johnston, a prominent member of the film industry's War Cooperation Committee and the editor of the trade magazine *Motion Picture News*. Framed as a series of questions, Johnston's letter relayed a number of industry complaints about the government's official film program. It catalogued the failure of the CPI's Division of Films in almost everything it had undertaken, hinting darkly that some of the division's staff might be reaping personal financial gains from their government service.[2]

Most of this suspicion was focused on Jules Brulator, the chairman of the CPI's Foreign Film Service and the man William Brady had appointed as chairman of the industry's short-lived American Cinema Commission. Creel had a long-standing relationship with both men. While working for Brady's World Film Corporation, Brulator participated in the production of *The Seats of the Mighty* (1914), a film in which Creel's wife, the stage star Blanche Bates, made her screen debut.[3] However, Brulator's subsequent employment as a salesman for the Eastman Kodak Company was the basis for industry concern.

One of Brulator's first tasks as director of the CPI Foreign Film Service was to collect educational films. With Creel's help, he convinced a number of companies, such as the Ford Motor Company, United States Steel, and International Harvester, to donate films which highlighted aspects of American business, agriculture and education. Although Johnston denigrated the value of this kind of film, what really upset him was the possibility that Brulator might be profiting personally from the sale of Kodak film stock used to print these films for the Foreign Film Service. He asked Creel to explain how the CPI selected its film laboratories and awarded its contracts. Johnston also criticized the film division's staff for its lack of production experience and suggested that the government's film program would be far better served by keeping charitable organizations like the Red Cross "out of the sphere of direct distribution."[4]

Figure 40. George Creel in Paris with the American Commission to Negotiate Peace, 1919. (Signal Corps Photo, National Archives)

Johnston was certainly right about the lack of experience on the CPI's film staff. Creel was a journalist by trade and his primary interest in motion pictures was that of a publicist. For Creel, the movies were another way of expanding the CPI's public relations effort. His film experience was limited at best. While working for the *Denver Post* in 1910, Creel had worked as an extra on several one-reel westerns with cowboy star G. M. Anderson, better known as "Bronco Billy" Anderson. Creel was so enamored with the work that summer that he wrote a few short scripts for Anderson for the sum of $25 each.[5]

Like Creel, the Division of Pictures' Rufus Steele was a writer who had published a number of articles in the *Saturday Evening Post*. Steele had produced a preparedness film, *The Eagle's Wings*, during the neutrality years and was better known in government circles than in the film industry. The same could be said of fellow staff member Laurence Rubel, who also made a preparedness film during the neutrality period. And both Steele and Rubel had more experience than the Division of Film's chairman, Louis Mack, who evidently had no involvement with motion pictures either before or after the First World War.

Mack's appointment with the Division of Film is probably the clearest indication of the limited role Creel initially envisioned for the CPI film effort. Creel's desire to avoid competition with existing film campaigns left Louis Mack with one basic task: funneling Signal Corps films free of charge to the Red Cross and state councils of defense. Here again, Johnston's criticism seems justified. Neither the Red Cross nor the state defense councils was a real film distributor and although the Signal Corps was just beginning to produce films, neither service organization possessed the resources to ensure that they would be widely seen.

In drafting a response to Johnston's letter, Creel, significantly, sought assistance from Laurence Rubel rather than Louis Mack. Rubel drafted a detailed reply to each of Johnston's questions, but when Creel answered Johnston's letter he ignored most of Rubel's research. Instead, he launched into a passionate defense of his friend Jules Brulator. Creel assured Johnston that Brulator had "nothing to do with either the selection of films, with the ordering of prints, or with the quantity of prints. . . ." Industrial films, he explained, had been collected by the Division of Films because the CPI's "representatives in foreign countries have asked for just such pictures, and I feel that these people who are on the ground, are in a better position to know the demands than anyone else."[6]

Creel's confident reply, however, could not really mask what had become obvious to everyone—the Division of Films was in shambles. Its entire program had been based on the full cooperation of the American film industry, a foundation which appeared to be crumbling amidst charges of CPI favoritism and bias. To make matters worse, the industry's official War Cooperation Committee, the Red Cross and the state councils of defense were spending more time squabbling over jurisdictional disputes than in making films or getting them shown to the American people. Even the Signal Corps' early efforts to produce a film history of the war had proven a disappointment. As Laurence Rubel confessed to Creel in January 1918, the CPI was "exceedingly embarrassed by lack of material with which to show, not only America, but to the world, that America *is* in the war, that she has *men* in France, and that they *are actually* doing something."[7]

The solution to these problems was a complete restructuring of the Division of Films. Louis Mack resigned as chairman on April 13, 1918, after receiving a telegram from Carl Byoir, the associate director of the CPI Foreign Section, who suggested that the "only patriotic thing" for Mack to do was to submit his resignation to Creel.[8] Even before Mack resigned, Creel had probably secured his replacement—Charles S. Hart, former advertising manager of *Hearst's Magazine*. Although the exact date when Hart began working for the Division of Films is unclear, Creel received a letter from William Randolph Hearst in early March 1918 begging him not to take Hart unless it was absolutely necessary.[9] For a short time, Hart evidently worked in the Division of Films' distribution unit, but even before Mack resigned, he had already begun to reorganize the Division of Films.

Under Hart's aggressive leadership the CPI greatly expanded its early film effort. One of Hart's first decisions was to move the division's main office from Washington to New York, a location which placed it nearer the film laboratories and distributing exchanges that the CPI worked with on a daily basis. Hart also developed a number of new subdivisions within the Division of Films, and replaced most of the staff appointed during Louis Mack's tenure as chairman. The permanent staff of the film division eventually exceeded forty-five people, a figure not including staff members who worked on the road or in the CPI's Foreign Film Service.[10]

Charles Hart had no prior motion picture experience before he became chairman of the Division of Films, but he quickly demonstrated some of the attributes of a fledgling movie mogul. Within a short time, he greatly expanded the CPI's ability to make and distribute films. Eventually, the Division of Films branched out into film exhibition, staging special screenings of CPI films at commercial movie theaters across the country. Hart, clearly, was no longer bound by Creel's directive to avoid competition with the private film industry. In fact, Hart's growing film program demanded an even greater level of industry-government cooperation. By the time the war ended, the Division of Films had become one of the largest and most successful areas within the entire Committee on Public Information.

**The Government Goes into the Movie Business**

By the time Charles Hart became chairman of the Division of Films, the Signal Corps' Photographic Section had solved many of its early problems and was beginning to send a steady supply of motion pictures to the United States. Creel was particularly anxious for this material to receive "100 per cent utilization."[11] Hart began building a staff of film editors, writers, and cameramen to supplement the work of the Signal Corps, and the CPI went into the business of making its own films. During the final six months of the war, the Division of Films produced a series of feature-length films such as *Pershing's Crusaders, America's Answer* and *Under Four Flags.* The division also produced several two-reel pictures, including *The U.S.A. Series* (four episodes), *Our Bridge of Ships,* and *Our Colored Fighters,* a film which highlighted the contributions of black Americans to the war effort.[12]

Compared to the melodramatic war films being released by the private film industry, the CPI's films were not particularly propagandistic. *Pershing's Crusaders,* the Division of Film's first feature-length film, is basically a compilation of Signal Corps news film. Its structure is episodic and, at times, confusing. The film opens with scenes of rubble in Belgium, the *Lusitania,* and captured German ships in New York. It seems to develop an argument justifying America's intervention in the war, but quickly dissolves to a tour of President Wilson's office, a survey of Liberty Loan statistics, and a sequence showing how Army shoes and clothing are made.[13]

Most of the overt propaganda in the CPI feature films was concentrated in the title cards or in patriotic prologues and epilogues. *America's Answer,* for example, begins with a tableau of flag-draped doughboys and a leering "Hun." It ends with the title *America's Answer* spelled out by hundreds of sailors who throw their white hats into the air.[14] To improve the title cards in the CPI feature films, Hart hired Bruce Barton, the editor of *Every Week* magazine. He explained Barton's duties in a letter:

> A big problem is to incorporate in these pictures some telling propaganda which at the same time would not be obvious propaganda but will have the effect we desire to create. We have been informed that you are the master of the short phrase and one of the best caption writers in the U. S.[15]

Basically these captions were caustic asides about "Huns," "The German Policy of the Broken Word," or "Just as the Kaiser's Hordes Fall," a title which appears just before a shot of Army lumberjacks felling a large tree. Ironically, the Signal Corps re-edited many of these films in 1936, and by simply omitting or modifying the titles it was an easy task to remove the anti-German elements from the CPI films. A 1936 title in *Pershing's Crusaders* reads: "Motor Trucks." In 1918, this title read: "Motor Trucks, an important link in the chain we are welding for the Kaiser and his sons."[16]

In addition to its feature film productions, the Division of Films began work on its most demanding film production assignment in the Great War, a weekly newsreel entitled the *Official War Review*. Each issue of the *Official War Review* was edited from a combination of footage supplied by the Army Signal Corps and the French, British, and Italian film services. Charles Urban, the man who had produced many of the "official" British films seen in the United States during the neutrality period, edited most of this material for the CPI. His primary assistant was Ray L. Hall, the first editor for the Hearst newsreel organization.[17]

Bringing together the different factions involved in the *Official War Review* was one of Hart's most difficult assignments. Each of the Allied film services had already developed its own system for exploiting war films in the United States. Although Allied films were usually sold to newsreel companies and distributed through regular commercial channels, the role of the American Red Cross complicated this situation. Even before the United States entered the war, the Red Cross had staged a number of lucrative benefit screenings for the French and British film services. After the American declaration of war, the Red Cross expanded this effort with the work of its own film production unit at the American Relief Clearing House in Paris. The CPI's initial agreement with the Red Cross acknowledged its dominating position. All Signal Corps films were funneled through the CPI to the Red Cross, which distributed them without charge to schools, churches and other organizations.

Hart knew that if the CPI hoped to produce the *Official War Review,* the Division of Films had to gain control of the foreign war films being shown in the United States. After several bitter meetings, Hart and Creel eventually persuaded Red Cross officials to turn all of their film activities over to the CPI film division.[18] Hart then turned his attention to the Allied film services. First, he began negotiations with Captain George Baynes, who controlled not only the British war pictures, but the *Italian Film Journal* as well. Baynes showed no interest in a joint newsreel with the CPI, and the CPI suspected that he might be trying to protect a lucrative deal set up with the Kineto Company, the laboratory responsible for printing his war films.[19] After a little checking, the CPI discovered that Baynes indeed had sold the rights to his films to the Kineto Company. Creel immediately contacted Kineto's president, and after an appeal to his patriotism, the CPI secured complete control of the British and Italian war pictures in the United States.[20]

The last hold-out was Edmund Ratisbonne, the head of the French Pictorial Service. Having obtained control of the British and Italian pictures, and with the Red Cross removed from the sphere of distribution and exhibition, Hart was in a position almost to dictate terms for a combined newsreel service:

> It is our opinion that the Official French War Pictures can be shown to much better advantage through this Official War Review than under your present arrangement. We realize the importance of the financial returns you are receiving at the present from the News Weeklies, and will arrange to pay you $400 a week during the life of this agreement for the exclusive rights to the weekly French pictures in the United States. The amount of footage to be devoted to the French pictures under this proposed arrangement would be determined by the interest of the pictures. However, we will agree that a minimum of 100 feet of French pictures will be used in each issue. [21]

Although the terms of this agreement were renegotiated several times during the war, the *Official War Review* substantially reduced the revenue for the Allied film services and turned most of the profits over to the CPI Division of Films. Within a matter of weeks Hart and Creel had gained almost total control of all war films in the United States, a domination so complete that even the commercial newsreel companies were forced to work through the Division of Films if they wanted to obtain war films. Later, as the Division of Films continued to expand its operations, this leverage proved invaluable.

Having secured the raw film footage necessary for a full-blown government film production effort, Hart began assembling a production staff with professional filmmaking experience. He hired Jane Stannard Johnson, the former advertising and publicity manager for Paramount Pictures, as production secretary. He also hired two experienced film editors from the Pathe newsreel organization, H. C. Hoagland and his longtime assistant Marie Ginoris. [22] Hart also began building a staff of cameramen: Albert Richard, Joseph Rucker, Robert Donahue, and two Signal Corps cinematographers, Lieutenant Edwin F. Weigle and Lieutenant W. H. Durborough. Both Weigle and Durborough had established their reputations as war cameramen prior to America's entry into the war. Weigle, it will be recalled, had shot many of the "official" films released by the *Chicago Tribune,* and Durborough had gone behind the German lines to shoot footage of the fall of Warsaw which was edited into *On the German Firing Line* (1915). [23]

Hart secured many of these new staff members through contacts in the private film industry, a procedure which enabled the CPI to help the Signal Corps obtain more experienced film personnel. Adolph Zukor, president of Paramount Pictures, worked with Creel to obtain a Signal Corps commission for one of his employees, Albert Kaufmann. Zukor also helped the Division of Films hire accountant Louis Loeb, the former comptroller at Paramount. [24]

Figure 41. Title card from the *Official War Review*. (Signal Corps Photo, National Archives)

As a means of shoring up the CPI's vital relationship with the film industry, Hart established several industry-based advisory committees to oversee the Division of Films. The first Advisory Committee was composed of the editors of the three leading industry trade magazines: Leslie Mason of the *Exhibitor's Trade Review*; James Hoff of *Moving Picture World*; and the man who was at least partially responsible for prodding the Division of Films into action, William Johnston from *Moving Picture News*.[25] Several months later, Hart formed an "Advisory Board of Motion Picture Directors" which was supposed to read and recommend screenplays for the Division of Films. Although there is nothing in the CPI records to indicate that the professional directors participated in any of the CPI productions, the establishment of the two advisory boards defused some of the industry's criticism and demonstrated the Division of Film's growing sophistication.[26]

Having assembled his staff and patched up the Division's faltering relationship with the film industry, Hart turned his attention towards the Signal Corps in France. Although the Corps' Photographic Section had now begun to produce a steady stream of films, there were often long delays before the films reached the CPI in the United States. In May 1918, Hart sent E. B. Hatrick, the CPI's film representative in France, on a tour of the Signal Corps' facilities. Hatrick, who had worked for years with the Hearst newsreel organization, made a number of suggestions for expediting the delivery of Signal Corps films to the Division of Films. What the Signal Corps needed most, he suggested, was "a capable film editor . . . who can handle the stuff as it comes in and who can eliminate a great deal of the bad material that goes through the laboratory and clogs up the works." He also recommended that the Signal Corps separate its efforts to shoot a military history of the war from its attempts to provide material for CPI propaganda films. By placing a CPI liaison officer with the Signal Corps Intelligence Section, Hatrick felt the Division of Films could speed up the censorship process and obtain the best film material at the same time. Furthermore, this liaison officer might be able to coordinate the work of special photographic units operating outside the Signal Corps' normal divisional structure.[27]

By the end of the war, the Signal Corps had adopted most of Hatrick's recommendations. Signal Corps films were funneled directly to the CPI through James Kearney, the CPI director in France. Films that had previously been sent by registered mail or diplomatic pouch were hand-carried to the U.S. by a CPI representative, a process which not only helped the Division of Films glean the best material out of the Signal Corps films, but reduced the lengthy delays caused by military censorship in Paris.[28] Several months before the war ended, the CPI placed film editor H. C. Hoagland with the Signal Corps Intelligence Section. Hoagland was given "large liberty of action" in the hope that his vast newsreel experience would result in "a strengthened propaganda service."[29]

Figure 42. At work in the Signal Corps photographic laboratory.
(Signal Corps Photo, National Archives)

Figure 43. Inspecting a roll of film in the Signal Corps laboratory.
(Signal Corps Photo, National Archives)

Although the CPI spent a great deal of time complaining about the Signal Corps' performance, the Corps' Photographic Section played a far greater role than is generally recognized in at least one of the CPI's feature film productions. In early March of 1918, Lieutenant Joe Marshall, the head of the Signal Corps Photographic Subsection, sent Captain Robert Warwick and Lieutenant Paul Miller to the Corps' Paris laboratory to assemble and title "a complete five-reel war film."[30] After completing the film, Warwick personally delivered it near the end of May to the War College. At that time, the CPI was engaged in the delicate negotiations over the *Official War Review*, and was also getting ready to release the Division of Film's first feature film, *Pershing's Crusaders*. Although Warwick wanted his film to be presented as a special Signal Corps production, CPI officials used it as the basis for *America's Answer*, the Division's second feature film.[31]

Warwick remained in Washington while the CPI's new production unit began reworking his film, adding titles and scenes of domestic mobilization activities. After watching an early version of *America's Answer*, Warwick complained to his commanding officer that the "titles lacked dignity and were not on par with the scope and breadth of the film."[32] Eventually, Warwick lodged a complaint with the industry-based CPI Advisory Board, and together they convinced the Division of Films to completely retitle *America's Answer* before it premiered at the Cohen Theatre in New York on July 29, 1918. Warwick, however, was never entirely satisfied with the CPI's version of the film, and he explained some of his misgivings in a note to his commanding officer:

> My only criticism of their arrangement of the film is their fear of presenting scenes which, in their opinion, were too morbid and might depress the public, such as a very impressive burial scene and several very striking hospital scenes. I disagree with them in this as I believe the seriousness of this war can only be brought home to them by the presentation of true details.[33]

The final step in the CPI's expanded film production effort was the creation of a new Scenario Department within the Division of Films. Louis Mack's original Scenario Department never got off the ground, and Hart asked Rufus Steele to establish a new, better department. Invoking the call of patriotism and government service, Steele immediately devised an irresistible plan to encourage private film companies to make films for the government. Steele's Scenario Department would write a script and secure all of the necessary government permits. In return, the private producer was given all commercial rights to the picture, a procedure which not only saved the CPI the expense of producing films, but guaranteed that Scenario Department productions would be widely distributed through regular commercial channels, since private producers would want not only to recoup their production expenses, but make a profit as well.[34]

Figure 44.  Sailors spelling out the title for *America's Answer*. (Post-Newsweek Television Stations, Inc. and Blackhawk Films)

By the end of the war eighteen one-reel pictures were completed through the Scenario Department's joint-production plan. The Pathe Company made two films as part of its "Winning the War" series: *Solving the Farm Problem in the Nation,* a film about the United States Boy's Working Reserve, and *Feeding the Fighter,* which focused on the work of the Army quartermaster and U.S. Food Administration. Universal also produced two films which were released under the general title "Wonders of Our War Work." The first of these films, *Reclaiming the Soldier's Duds,* showed the conservation efforts of the Army quartermaster. Universal's *The American Indian Gets into the War* portrayed the patriotic activities of American Indians, an effort which Steele felt "shamed the white man into a higher patriotism."[35] Paramount-Bray Pictograph made four films in its "Says Uncle Sam" series: *Keep 'Em Singing and Nothing Can Lick 'Em,* which explained the importance of vocal music in the military; *I'll Help Every Willing Worker Find a Job,* a film about the U. S. Employment Service; *A Girl's a Man for A' That and A' That,* which highlighted women's war work; and *I Run the Biggest Life Insurance Company on Earth,* a film about the government's War Risk Insurance Bureau.[36]

Virtually all of these films were newsreel-style documentaries, but occasionally actors were used to add interest. Unfortunately, not one of these films survives under its original title in the Signal Corps film collection at the National Archives. Films made in conjunction with the Scenario Department became the property of the producer and, to further complicate matters, the Signal Corps re-edited most of its films in 1936. There is no way of knowing for certain if the two extant films about War Risk Insurance in the Signal Corps collection were edited out of Paramount's *I Run the Biggest Life Insurance Company on Earth,* but these films probably indicate the kind of pictures produced under the auspices of the CPI Scenario Department.

*War Risk Insurance* (Signal Corps Historical Film 1195) is documentary in nature. It contains scenes of Secretary McAdoo issuing the first insurance certificates, a mechanical check-signing device, and pictures of officials from the War Risk Insurance Bureau. In contrast, *His Best Gift* (Signal Corps Historical Film 1542) uses actors to drive home the need to buy war insurance. A young soldier who has just gotten married forgets to buy war insurance. In a particularly vivid nightmare, he is blinded in battle and led helplessly to his front door, his eyes and face covered with bandages. A huge glycerin tear is running down his wife's face when he abruptly wakes up, utterly sold on the need to take out war risk insurance.

The private producer who took greatest advantage of the Scenario Department's services was C. L. Chester, a filmmaker who had built his career on short travel pictures and educational films. In the closing months of the war Chester produced a series of ten one-reel pictures which focused on

HER PROBLEM,

HUSBAND BLIND,

NO INSURANCE.

Figures 45, 46, and 47.  In sequence, the wife in *His Best Gift* learns
about her husband's failure to buy War
Risk Insurance.
(Post-Newsweek Television Stations, Inc. and
Blackhawk Films)

various military training procedures and domestic wartime activities. Chester also made a six-reel film, *The Miracle of the Ships,* which followed the construction of a ship from the steel mines and forests to the Navy shipyard at Hog Island.[37]

By far the longest and most expensive film made through the Scenario Department was *Made in America,* an eight-reel picture produced by the W. W. Hodkinson Corporation at a cost exceeding forty thousand dollars. It showed how military men were drafted, trained and sent into combat overseas. The film was not finished when the armistice was signed, but Hodkinson completed it anyway. In February of 1919, he showed the film to a gathering of dignitaries at the War College in Washington, and a print of the film was sent to General Pershing in France.[38]

Shortly before the war ended, Rufus Steele radically expanded the scope of the Scenario Department's operations. The department began to write scripts and make films without the help of commercial producers. The CPI Records offer no explanation for this change in procedure, but in the closing days of the war the Scenario Department completed six two-reel films in this manner: *If Your Soldier's Hit, Our Wings of Victory, Our Horses of War, Making the Nation Fit, The Storm of Steel* and *The Bath of Bullets.* The Scenario Department did not begin releasing these films until December 23, 1918 and two films, *Bath of Bullets* and *Storm of Steel,* were never shown to the public. The CPI had been completely disbanded before they could be exhibited.[39]

Had the First World War not ended as soon as it did, it is possible that the Scenario Department might have established the U. S. government as a major film producer. Nevertheless, in six short months, Charles Hart had transformed the Division of Films from a secondhand film distributor to an increasingly capable film production agency. During his brief tenure as chairman, the Division of Films produced or sponsored sixty-six government motion pictures, including thirty-one episodes of the *Official War Review.* Only the signing of the armistice on November 11, 1918, kept this activity from expanding further.

## Distribution and Exhibition

The Division of Films was created primarily for the purpose of distributing Signal Corps films to various patriotic and educational organizations. Much of this work had been handed over to the American Red Cross and state councils of defense, but by the time Charles Hart became division chairman, the CPI's distribution effort was, in George Creel's words, "failing absolutely to place the pictorial record of America's war progress before more than a small percentage of the motion picture audiences of the world."[40]

Writing in the twenties, film historian Terry Ramsaye provided a perceptive analysis of the CPI's distribution problems: a government press release was far different from a free government motion picture. The CPI's press corps could get a story published in any newspaper in the country, but the only way to be sure a CPI film message would reach the American public was for the film to be distributed and exhibited through regular industry channels.[41]

As the CPI expanded its film production effort, the distribution problem became even more acute. Not only was distribution of free films ineffective, but it was, ironically, expensive as well. The Committee's desire to provide free films for use in foreign countries put an even greater demand on the Division of Films to put income back in the CPI's till. Again, the CPI turned to the private film industry for assistance.

As Hart reorganized the Division of Films, he made a close examination of the system devised by the American Red Cross for distributing war films to the different newsreel companies. What he discovered was a distribution scheme the CPI definitely did not want to follow:

> The method of distribution by the editors of the four weeklies was determined as follows. When film is received from the Red Cross the four editors of Pathe, Universal, Mutual and Gaumont divide the weekly supply into four packages, one for each company. Then they hold a dice-throwing contest, the winner having first choice, the second highest man second selection, etc. In other words, the News Weeklies do not duplicate pictures. The Red Cross recently had the first pictures showing the operation of liquid gas. This prize of the night was won by Universal which has half the circulation of Pathe. Consequently this important picture for propaganda was distributed only in a limited way.[42]

After the Division of Films wrested control of war films from the Red Cross and Allied film services, it had almost cornered the market for war films in the United States. Hart's initial offer to the four newsreel companies reflects his dominant position and showed how far the government film effort had come from the Red Cross dice-rolling scheme. He offered the newsreel companies two thousand feet of war film at a flat rate of $5,000 per week.[43] This plan fell apart when one of the companies, probably Universal, not only refused to participate, but suggested that the government should give them the war films at no cost.

By the time negotiations ended, the Division of Films had decided to use the war films in its own newsreel production, the *Official War Review*. Now Hart needed a distributor rather than a production company. He offered to sell the *War Review* to any of the four commercial newsreel companies, and after a bitter bidding war, the powerful Pathe Company, the largest newsreel organization, won the rights to distribute the official government newsreel. Under the contract terms, Pathe agreed to return 80 percent of the proceeds

Figure 48.   Navy band marching in the CPI's *Official War Review.*
(Post-Newsweek Television Stations, Inc. and Blackhawk
Films)

from the *Official War Review* to the Division of Films. Later in the war, when it became apparent that the *Official War Review* was not exhausting the supply of war films, the CPI agreed to provide a weekly quota of five hundred feet of film to each of the four newsreel companies. For this service, each company paid the fee of one dollar per foot of film.[44]

The CPI feature films posed a different distribution problem. It was one thing to get the newsreel companies to distribute a short government newsreel which could be shown on the same film program with the industry's normal feature films, and another to convince commercial film distributors to handle a feature-length film that took up the entire program. Hart knew he had to make the CPI feature films more marketable, and he fell back on a sales technique which had been perfected on the preparedness films in the neutrality period—prerelease screenings accompanied by a massive publicity campaign. These "official screenings" brought the Division of Films into the sphere of direct exhibition. To coordinate this new effort, Hart secured the services of George Bowles, the man who had handled foreign distribution for Griffith's *Birth of a Nation.* Bowles established eight road companies, each with its own business, sales and advertising representatives. These companies concentrated entirely on large metropolitan areas, staging "official screenings" for *Pershing's Crusaders* in twenty-four cities, *America's Answer* in thirty-four, and *Under Four Flags* (which was released after the armistice) in nine.[45]

Each "official screening" lasted for approximately one week. The film was shown in either a commercial movie house or a large municipal auditorium which the CPI rented. To publicize the film, the CPI enlisted the support of local business organizations, social clubs and patriotic societies. Occasionally, the entire theater would be sold to a single group which would help the CPI advertise the film by distributing window cards, posters and banners throughout the community. This work was backed up by a full-scale publicity campaign directed by Marcus A. Beeman from the CPI's Washington office. Before a CPI feature film opened, telegrams were sent to every movie critic in the town, asking them to help stimulate interest in the picture. In addition, a vast array of advertising material was mailed out to newspapers, magazines and motion picture trade papers. The CPI also secured endorsements from local officials, and by staging special Washington screenings, the committee soon discovered that it could incorporate favorable comments from members of Congress and the president into its publicity materials.[46]

It was Creel's hope that these prerelease screenings would have "an impressiveness that would lift them out of the class of ordinary motion pictures. . . ."[47] The CPI feature films were shown in theaters decorated with flags, bunting and patriotic paintings. Opening nights, in particular, were turned into gala war rallies, with invitations sent to government officials, members of visiting war missions, movie stars, and prominent men and women in the community. A fifty-man choir from the Pelham Bay Naval Station opened the New York premiere of *America's Answer* by singing "The Star Spangled Banner," and during the intermission, George Creel delivered a rousing speech in which he explained the purpose of the film and the importance of the CPI film effort.[48]

The second phase of Hart's feature distribution plan involved placing the CPI's films in the hands of commercial distributors, a process made far easier by the "official screenings," the celebrity endorsements, and the massive publicity campaign. With the exception of three states—Michigan, North Dakota, and California—where the CPI's films were distributed by the state councils of defense, all of the Division's feature-length films were distributed on a regular percentage basis by commercial distributors.[49] This activity was coordinated by a Bureau of Distribution within the Division of Films. Dennis J. Sullivan and George Meeker served as directors and as their division expanded they placed sales representatives in seventeen cities to encourage distribution and work out booking problems.[50]

With Hart's urging, the trade magazine *Moving Picture World* organized a contest in which an ornate bronze trophy was awarded to the film exchange booking *Pershing's Crusaders* into the largest number of theaters within a territorial district. After the contest, which was won by the Denver exchange, *Moving Picture World* claimed that *Pershing's Crusaders* had received "the most comprehensive bookings ever made for a film of any description."[51]

To encourage the sale of the committee's features in rural areas, the Bureau of Distribution developed a proportionate rental plan based on the average income derived from a particular theater. When the CPI discovered that a few exhibitors had raised ticket prices for *Pershing's Crusaders*, it began inserting a clause in its feature film contracts which stipulated that an exhibitor would not increase admission prices during the showing of any government film.[52]

The overwhelming success of Hart's distribution plan can readily be demonstrated by the number of bookings the Division of Films secured for its films:

| | |
|---|---|
| *Official War Review* (31 issues) | 6,950 bookings |
| *Pershing's Crusaders* | 4,189 bookings |
| *America's Answer* | 4,548 bookings |
| *Under Four Flags* | 1,820 bookings |
| *U.S.A. Series* (4 subjects) | 212 bookings[53] |

George Creel estimated that the CPI films played in 40 percent of the twelve thousand motion picture theaters in the United States. In some cases, this figure went even higher. *America's Answer* was booked into 60 percent of the theaters in the New York City area. Considering the proximity of theaters in most large cities, the CPI was probably correct in its claim that the government's motion pictures had received nearly 100 percent distribution in the United States.[54]

The income from these bookings nearly enabled the Division of Films to break even, even though the CPI continued to furnish free films to military training camps, schools, hospitals, patriotic societies and the Foreign Film Service. The Division's total expenditures came to $1,066,730 and over 75 percent of this cost was returned through the sale or rental of CPI films:

| | |
|---|---|
| *Pershing's Crusaders* | $181,741 |
| *America's Answer* | $185,144 |
| *Under Four Flags* | $ 63,946 |
| *Official War Review* | $334,622 |
| *U.S.A. Series* | $ 13,864 |
| *Our Bridge of Ships* | $    922 |
| *Our Colored Fighters* | $    640 |
| *News Weekly* | $ 15,150 |
| Miscellaneous Sales | $ 56,641 |
| Total Sales | $852,744[55] |

Under Hart's leadership, the Division of Films far surpassed any previous government attempt to use motion pictures in an official capacity. By the time the First World War ended, United States government films were being shown in every state of the union and over sixty-two hundred reels of government pictures had been shipped abroad. This transformation had taken place in slightly less than seven months. From its rocky beginnings under Louis Mack, the Division of Films had evolved into one of the largest and most important divisions within the entire Committee on Public Information.

None of the CPI's films will be mistaken for landmarks of cinematic art nor will they be remembered as shining examples of government documentary filmmaking. The CPI film production effort was developed too hastily and too haphazardly to reach those heights. There is little evidence, in fact, to suggest that the CPI actually spent much time planning its films. To a great extent, the Division of Films was at the mercy of Signal Corps cameramen who were shooting their film for entirely different purposes. It is not hard to envision the CPI film editing staff late at night, trying desperately to figure out some way to use a Signal Corps "record film" showing how the Army recycled shoes. Perhaps the work of the Scenario Department, which wrote and produced six short films near the end of the war, would have changed the

Figures 49 and 50.  Animated Signal Corps film warning soldiers
about the dangers of joy-riding and the results
of going AWOL.
(Post-Newsweek Television Stations, Inc. and
Blackhawk Films)

thrust of the CPI film production program, but with so little opportunity to coordinate the work of cinematographers and editors, the CPI's films were compilation films with the emphasis on "compilation."

In any case, Charles Hart's greatest achievement was not in making government films, but in getting them shown to a tremendous percentage of the American people. With the crucial assistance of the private film industry, the Division of Films made it possible for all Americans to see government pictures in their neighborhood theaters, an effort unmatched until the Second World War. Having entered the commercial marketplace, the CPI discovered, perhaps surprisingly, that even government films could make money. Without the drain of distribution of free films at home and abroad, the Division of Films would have made back the money it spent, and more. As it was, the Division of Films was one of few areas in the CPI that was close to self-sustaining.

The key to the government's entire World War I film program was the support provided by the American film industry. Without access to commercial movie theaters, Hart's expanded film effort could never have taken place. Many months after the war had ended, industry spokesmen complained that their companies had been damaged because the United States government had gone into direct competition with their newsreel organizations.[56] With so many areas of potential conflict, it is surprising that this kind of complaint was heard so rarely during the First World War.

Most film companies seem to have gone out of their way to demonstrate their patriotism and support for the government's film campaign. The relatively short duration of CPI film activity probably helped reduce friction between the industry and the government. Government documentaries and newsreels may have been an inconvenience, but it is doubtful if they really interfered with the industry's primary theatrical film business. The real threat to the film industry, as we shall see, was not in competition from the Division of Films, but in the regulatory power of the federal government. Although George Creel fostered the image of a smiling public relations man, he was not timid about using government regulations to expand the CPI's film program or to encourage the film industry's continuing support.

Figure 51. Animated sequence from an industry-produced war newsreel. (Post-Newsweek Television Stations, Inc. and Blackhawk Films)

## 5

# Government Controls and the Industry's Quest for Acceptance

In his writings about the Committee on Public Information, George Creel consistently understated the CPI's involvement in censorship:

> In no degree was the Committee an agency of censorship, a machinery of concealment or repression. Its emphasis throughout was on the open and positive. At no point did it seek or exercise authorities under those laws that limited the freedom of speech and press. In all things, from first to last, without halt or change, it was a plain publicity proposition, a vast enterprise in salesmanship, the world's greatest adventure in advertising.[1]

Although this statement accurately reflects Creel's primary interest—the dissemination of government news and publicity—it is also misleading. The CPI was created with the understanding that it would combine the functions of censorship and publicity within a single agency, and as the war continued, the U.S. government developed a formidable array of censorship powers through a combination of federal statutes and executive orders. The Espionage Act of June 15, 1917, the Trading-with-the-Enemy Act of October 6, 1917, and the Sedition Act of May 1918 provided the federal government with the means to regulate virtually every form of communication, whether written, spoken or filmed, whether transmitted by wireless, cable or mail.[2] The Department of Justice and the Post Office Department were the government agencies officially charged with enforcing these statutes. But through his contacts with those departments and his relationship with Army and Navy Intelligence, Creel was in a position to exert considerable influence over wartime censorship.[3]

Creel was also a member of the Censorship Board, established by President Wilson (through Executive Order 2729-A) on October 12, 1917 as a means of coordinating the government's different censorship agencies. In addition to Creel, who represented the CPI, the Censorship Board included representatives from the secretary of war (Brigadier General Frank McIntyre), the postmaster general (Robert L. Maddox and Eugene Russell), and the War Trade Board (Paul Fuller, Jr.). Creel was not the dominant force on the Censorship Board, but he was an active participant in its discussions and recommendations.[4]

Creel's inside knowledge of censorship policy enabled the CPI to become deeply involved in film censorship and film export controls. By the time the war ended, the United States government possessed perhaps the greatest power it had ever possessed to regulate the content of American motion pictures.

## Domestic Film Censorship

Technically, the CPI had no statutory censorship authority. Nevertheless, the Committee and its representatives could exert pressure on filmmakers that was very close to direct censorship. A case in point was the so-called "voluntary censorship" plan that the CPI worked out with the newsreel companies early in the war. In order to shoot film at any military installation, newsreel companies were forced to obtain a permit from the CPI's Division of Pictures. After the film had been shot, it was reviewed by the CPI in conjunction with Army and Navy Intelligence to determine if it compromised military security. Pictures made in this manner could not be exhibited without a release from the CPI.[5] If a film company ignored these procedures, the Justice Department—not the CPI—was called in to seize the film; this technicality allowed the CPI to claim that it was merely an intermediary between the film companies and the various government agencies actually responsible for enforcing censorship regulations.[6]

The CPI's role in theatrical film censorship involved what Creel also would have called a "voluntary censorship" pattern. One of the first examples of this kind of informal censorship involved President Wilson, and this case may have provided a precedent for the CPI's domestic film censorship during the war. The Hearst International Film Company had started releasing a fifteen-part preparedness serial entitled *Patria* in January of 1917. *Patria* developed the preparedness theme by portraying a ruthless Mexican-Japanese invasion of the United States, and Hearst International was still releasing new episodes of the serial when the United States entered the First World War.[7] The president had seen several episodes of the serial and after receiving complaints from Japanese Ambassador Hanrihara and from American Secretary of Commerce William Redfield, Wilson wrote a letter to the Hearst organization:[8]

> Several times in attending Keith's theatre I have seen portions of a film entitled *Patria*, which has been exhibited here and I think in a great many other theatres in the country. May I now say to you that the character of the story disturbed me very much. It is extremely

unfair to the Japanese, and I fear that it is calculated to stir up a great deal of hostility which will be far from beneficial to the country, indeed will, particularly in the present circumstances, be extremely hurtful. I take the liberty, therefore, of asking whether the Company would not be willing to withdraw it if it is still being exhibited.[9]

Although Wilson possessed no legal basis for interference, producer J.A. Berst agreed to revise the serial, reminding the president that the film represented an investment of nearly three-quarters of a million dollars and that Hearst International could not afford to withdraw it completely.[10]

After reworking the film, Berst submitted it to the White House. His changes, however, did not really satisfy the president, who wrote again, asking him to "omit all those scenes in which anything Japanese appears, particularly those showing the Japanese and Mexican armies invading the United States, pillaging homes, kidnapping women and committing all sorts of offenses."[11] Berst went back to work on the film and produced a new version. Although the president still felt that it contained objectionable material, he eventually rescinded his objections and allowed the film to be put back into commercial distribution.[12]

On at least two occasions during the First World War, the CPI censored films in precisely the same manner. The first case centered on *The Curse of Iku,* a film released by the Essanay Film Company in March 1918. Set in Japan in the 1850s, *The Curse of Iku* presented a complicated melodrama about a shipwrecked American sailor, a beautiful Oriental girl, and a barbaric Japanese villain named Iku. After receiving several letters claiming that the film was stirring up anti-Japanese feelings in California, the CPI secured a print of the film and reviewed it with representatives from the War Department and the State Department's Division of Far Eastern Affairs. Eventually, Essanay was persuaded to recall all prints of the film, to change all of the characters from Japanese to obscure Pacific islanders. The film was also renamed *An Eye for an Eye.*[13]

The second case of CPI "voluntary censorship" involved the Fox Film Company's *The Caillaux Case,* a film based on the life of the celebrated French statesman and the sensational murder trial of his wife. After seeing advertisements for the film in the Washington newspapers, the French High Commission lodged a protest with the CPI even before the film was released in April of 1918.[14] Again, the CPI obtained a print of the film and screened it with representatives of the French High Commission, and the Departments of State and War. It took Fox more than four months to re-edit the film to the CPI's specifications. Although these changes eventually satisfied the French, a letter to Creel from the State Department's Phillip H. Patchin suggests that Fox's revisions had not done much to help the film viewers who were going to see *The Caillaux Case* in their local theaters:

Now that they have it finished I find myself wondering what they are going to do with it. The only good stuff was objectionable and I am afraid there is not much left. It was a 7,000 foot film, or thereabouts, and it seems to me that fully 2,000 feet must have been titles with all the fireworks eliminated. It seems to me that patrons of the Fox Film Company might be saved a lot of trouble if the Company would simply print the titles, give them to their customers and let it go at that.[15]

The CPI's involvement in censorship of this kind was the exception rather than the rule. In fact, in World War I domestic film censorship was usually applied more harshly and more capriciously on the state or local level. In the spring of 1917, for example, a Pittsburgh film exhibitor was arrested and held under $5,000 bail for distributing handbills for Vitagraph's *The Battle Cry of Peace,* a film which had been attacked during the neutrality years for advocating American military preparedness. Pittsburgh authorities, however, felt that the handbills advertising the film were enough to discourage enlistment.[16] Though the statutory authority for this action was questionable, the motion pictures never enjoyed the same First Amendment protection as the press. With the nation at war, it is hardly surprising that state and municipal censorship boards would consider it their patriotic duty to govern the political content of motion pictures.

Commercial motion pictures were censored by a number of cities and states during the war years.[17] In Pennsylvania, Attorney General Francis S. Brown warned theater owners that their business licenses could be revoked if they showed films that discouraged recruitment or patriotism. Brown also sent letters to the producers of *Civilization* and *War Brides,* two pacifist war dramas made prior to American entry into the war, warning them not to release their films in Pennsylvania during the crisis.[18]

Perhaps the single most famous case of World War I film censorship took place in California. Robert Goldstein, the costume designer for D. W. Griffith's *The Birth of a Nation,* had produced a film entitled *The Spirit of '76.* He opened the film in Chicago in the summer of 1917 and it immediately ran into trouble with Major L. C. Funkhouser, the dictatorial Chicago police censor. Funkhouser suppressed the film on the grounds that it was excessively violent, particularly in its graphic portrayal of British atrocities at the Wyoming Valley Massacre. Goldstein obtained an injunction, and after a two-week trial in the Superior Court of Cook County, Illinois, he won the right to exhibit his film.[19]

Goldstein then moved west with his film, leaving Chicago with a reported debt of $35,000. He arranged a booking for *The Spirit of '76* at Clune's Auditorium in Los Angeles. Due to the controversy surrounding the film, he was required to show the film to a Los Angeles citizens group, which recommended that he remove several scenes. What this reviewing committee did not know, however, was that Goldstein had already removed the most controversial material prior to the screening, and he put it all back in for *The*

*Spirit of '76*'s Los Angeles opening. Acting under the authority of Title XI of the Espionage Act, District Attorney Robert O'Connor seized the film. The next day, Goldstein was arrested.[20]

In the case *United States v. the Motion Picture Film "The Spirit of '76,"* Judge Benjamin F. Bledsoe (U. S. District Court, Los Angeles) held that the film contained "exaggerated scenes of British cruelty," and that exhibition of the film would sow dissension and interfere with the war effort. Goldstein appealed the case, but the Circuit Court of Appeals affirmed the lower court's ruling. Goldstein was convicted on two counts of knowingly attempting to cause disloyalty or insubordination among the military forces, a violation of the Espionage Act of 1917 (Section 3 of Title 1). He was sentenced to ten years in the federal penitentiary and fined $10,000.[21]

President Wilson commuted Goldstein's sentence after the war, but the message to American filmmakers during the war years was unmistakably clear: this was not the time to make a film which seemed to discourage enlistment or patriotism. Whether the watchful eyes were those of the president, local military authorities, censorship boards, the CPI or extra-governmental organizations such as the National Security League, most filmmakers seemed well aware of the kind of films that were likely to be frowned upon. In fact, the omnipresent threat of censorship may have contributed, inadvertently, to the film industry's production of rabidly anti-German films such as *The Kaiser, the Beast of Berlin* or *My Four Years in Germany*. A film producer wanting to set a film against the backdrop of World War I was clearly on far safer ground portraying German atrocities than dealing with any story about the French or British. The CPI did not receive any letters complaining about films which distorted German ideals or slandered the German people. No one accused anti-German "hate" films of giving aid to the enemy.

As a result, the CPI seldom had any reason to censor films shown in the American market during the First World War. Although the CPI's role in domestic film censorship was limited, its involvement with films being shipped abroad was not. As the First World War continued, the CPI used film export restrictions not only to govern film content, but as a means of "encouraging" the American film industry to participate in the government's foreign film campaign.

## Export Controls

From the very beginning of the war George Creel showed a special interest in using motion picture propaganda abroad. The movies spoke an international language, and compared to modern sound films, the silent motion picture was relatively easy to adapt for propaganda purposes. It was a simple task to translate title cards, put them on film, and insert them into a foreign language version of a film. Jules Brulator, the head of the CPI's Foreign Film Service, had already collected and retitled a number of educational and industrial films, and as the Division of Films began to expand its production effort, he started to build a foreign distribution network. To facilitate this work, the Foreign Film Service placed staff members in a number of countries, including Russia, Argentina, China, Brazil, Peru, Bolivia, Ecuador, Mexico, Spain, France, Holland, Switzerland, and the Scandinavian countries. In Russia and China, CPI personnel put their films and projectors on a truck or train and traveled through the countryside giving shows in the rural villages and towns. In the more developed countries, CPI representatives either rented a local movie house or found a sympathetic theater owner willing to run the films. To Creel's chagrin, however, foreign film exhibitors, particularly in the neutral European countries, showed almost no interest in the CPI's growing stockpile of "educational" films. To make matters even worse, in Scandinavia and Switzerland, where the Germans exerted considerable influence, movie audiences often watched American-made theatrical films and German propaganda films on the same theater program.[22]

To remedy this situation, Creel devised a brilliant scheme which not only kept foreign exhibitors from showing German films, but forced many of them to show U. S. government films as part of their regular program. Through his work with Paul Fuller, Jr., the War Trade Board representative on the Censorship Board, Creel knew that the War Trade Board required every American exporter to secure an export license. Creel wrote Fuller on January 14, 1918, outlining a plan which used the War Trade Board's licensing requirements as a means of expanding the work of the CPI's Foreign Film Service:

> As you know we are trying to use the embargo for the development of our educational film work in foreign countries. Already three of the big agencies doing business in Sweden have taken our complete program as part of their shipments, and will show American pictures with their usual features.
>
> Will you be kind enough to take this matter up with the man who has charge of these motion picture licenses, and ask him to issue no licence until the application has been referred to us. In this way, we can get our material included in all foreign programs.[23]

Within the month the War Trade Board approved Creel's plan. Film exporters were required not only to secure a Trade Board license, but to obtain a certificate of approval from the CPI, a procedure which piggybacked government films through the film industry's foreign distribution network. In order to receive a CPI certificate, film exporters had to agree that at least 20 percent of every shipment would be made up of CPI "educational" films. Furthermore, no American films of any kind could be shipped to a foreign exhibitor who continued running German films or who refused to show the CPI's films.[24]

The CPI certificate plan exerted enormous pressure on European film exhibitors. They desperately needed the popular American entertainment films to make up for an acute shortage of domestic film products. In order to obtain those films, theater owners were forced to stop using German films and to run at least some of the CPI's films instead. Thus, as Creel later bragged, "Charlie Chaplin and Mary Pickford led *Pershing's Crusaders* and *America's Answer* into the enemy's territory and smashed another Hindenburg line."[25]

Within weeks German films were virtually pushed off the screen in Sweden and Norway and by the end of the war, the CPI's foreign film program had made significant inroads in Switzerland and Holland, countries where the Germans had previously dominated the film market.[26]

For a time, evidently, films that were being sent abroad were inspected twice, once for the War Trade Board export license and again for the CPI certificate. Eventually all export censorship was combined. The task of screening and censoring every foot of film that left the United States was enormous, and the majority of censors were actually supplied by the Army, Navy and Customs Department, rather than the CPI. By May 1918, however, the CPI had progressed far beyond the original War Trade Board mandate to keep materials that might be valuable out of the enemy's hands. A statement by Creel indicates the path the CPI export censorship eventually followed:

> It was not only that the Committee put motion pictures into foreign countries. Just as important was the work of keeping certain motion pictures out of these countries. As a matter of bitter fact, much of the misconception about America before the war was due to American motion pictures portraying the lives and exploits of New York's gun-men, Western bandits, and the wild days of the old frontier, all of which were accepted in many parts of the world as representative of American life.
>
> What we wanted to get into foreign countries were pictures that presented the wholesome life of America, giving fair ideas of our people and institutions. What we wanted to keep out of world circulation were the "thrillers" that gave entirely false impressions of American life and morals. Film dramas portraying the life of "Gyp the Blood," or "Jesse James," were bound to prejudice our fight for the good public opinion of the neutral nations.[27]

The CPI, obviously, had come a long way from its "voluntary censorship" plans. Operating out of customs offices in a number of port cities, censors from the Army, Navy, Customs Department and CPI began withholding export licenses for films because they did not foster the "proper" image of the United States.

The censor's cards in the CPI Records indicate some of the different reasons films were rejected. For example, the Jewell Company's *A Soul for Sale* was turned down by the CPI censor on the following grounds: "Gives a very objectionable view of life: A mother trying to sell her daughter, the mother forging an order for jewelry which implicates the daughter; gambling scenes in an American country house."[28] A number of westerns were rejected for dealing with Mexican bandits or Mexican border incidents, as were films

Figure 52.  Actress Mary Pickford works the crowd at a Liberty
Loan rally.
(Post-Newsweek Television Stations, Inc. and Blackhawk
Films)

Figure 53.  Title card showing that a film has been passed by the
CPI.
(Post-Newsweek Television Stations, Inc. and Blackhawk
Films)

that dealt with the Civil War or slavery. By my count, approximately eight thousand films were checked over in this manner and only one hundred were actually denied an export license.[29]

On the surface, those numbers suggest that the CPI's export censorship was neither very harsh, nor very important. Although it is extremely difficult to find reliable statistics concerning the film business in this period, a 1916 staff memorandum from the Price, Waterhouse Accounting Company suggests that the export sales for an American film could make up as much as 30 percent of a film's earnings. Price, Waterhouse also predicted that within just a few years, almost no American films could make a profit without export earnings.[30] If the export market was that important to American film companies in 1917, the CPI's export certificate plan provided the government with extraordinary power.

In an age of skyrocketing salaries and higher production costs, the film business had become more risky than before the war. An extremely popular film like *The Birth of a Nation* might make a profit in just the American market, but few film manufacturers would have been willing to risk the loss of the all-important foreign market. As a result, the CPI certificate plan may have acted as a form of prior restraint in the domestic market, discouraging the production of films that seemed likely to incur the government's wrath.

In an effort to clarify the CPI's ever-expanding export regulations, William Brady, the head of the film industry's War Cooperation Committee and the president of the National Association of the Motion Picture Industry, arranged a meeting between CPI Associate Director Carl Byoir and the NAMPI's Paul Cromelin in early July of 1918. One outcome of this meeting was a set of guidelines pertaining to export film censorship. American film companies were warned not to make pictures which impugned American ideals or life, denigrated the U.S. or its Allies, or gave comfort to the enemy. This meeting also provided several important concessions for the American film industry. Censorship was lifted from films being shipped to Great Britain and France or their colonies, provided the exporter could assure the CPI that the films would not be re-exported to a neutral country. Even more important was a redefinition of the term "educational" film. Prior to the meeting the CPI had classified only government films, newsreels, travelogues and industrial films as "educational." This definition was broadened to include the industry's regular entertainment films provided that they gave "some idea of American life and purpose."[31]

Perhaps the most surprising thing about the CPI's export censorship plan was the almost total lack of industry response. Given the film industry's frantic prewar publicity campaign against federal film censorship, the CPI records do not indicate that filmmakers protested against these restraints. Of course, much of this activity was begun late in the war, but outside of some criticism in Congress, where Creel had a number of long-standing enemies, the CPI's film program came under serious attack only once during the entire First World War.

## Congressional Scrutiny and the Universal Affair

For three days, beginning June 11, 1918, Creel and CPI Associate Director Carl Byoir appeared before the House Committee on Appropriations. The expanded activities of the CPI Film Division received particularly close scrutiny. Creel gave the Appropriations Committee a complete list of CPI employees and their salaries, but he was unable to provide a complete accounting of CPI production costs since he did not know what the Signal Corps spent to shoot its productions. What really seemed to upset the Appropriations Committee was the revelation that CPI films produced with government funding were being sold for profit. Representative Swagar Shirley, chairman of the Appropriations Committee, asked Creel to explain why this profit-making venture could not be turned over to the private film industry. Creel argued that the money made from a film like *Pershing's Crusaders* did not really represent a profit, since all income was used to defray CPI production costs and to underwrite free film distribution at home and abroad.[32]

The results of Creel's appearance before the Appropriations Committee were mixed. Creel felt that the hearings had given him the opportunity to win the "respect and approval" of both Democrats and Republicans in the House, but this approval did not extend to the Committee's purse strings. His funding request was slashed by 40 percent, a decision which inadvertently placed even greater demands on the Division of Films to make money with its films.[33] The funding bill also included a provision banning payments to any draft-age men, a ruling which affected between fifteen and twenty CPI employees, including Associate Director Byoir. Although Creel eventually obtained a special deferment for Byoir, the CPI was forced to cut back on some of its activities.[34]

The goodwill Creel felt he had established with Congress began to unravel just five days later. At hearings on the motion picture war tax before the House Ways and Means Committee, Patrick A. Powers, treasurer of the Universal Film Manufacturing Company, launched a spectacular attack on the Division of Films and plunged the CPI into the most serious controversy it faced during the World War. Powers accused the Committee of giving the Hearst-Pathe Newsreel organization a complete monopoly of Signal Corps films in the United States. He also claimed that the government treated Hearst-Pathe with special deference because of the large number of Hearst employees working within the CPI's Division of Films.[35] There was probably a personal side to Power's attack. His relationship with Creel and the CPI had been acrimonious long before the Ways and Means hearings. Powers had been appointed to the industry-based American Cinema Commission, but when the CPI created its Foreign Film Service, using most of the industry's appointees for staff, Powers was pointedly omitted. Powers had also been involved in a heated dispute with Raymond B. Fosdick, the head of the War Department's Commission on Training Camp Activities. Fosdick and Powers had developed conflicting plans for showing films at military installations. Fosdick, in anger, wrote a letter to President Wilson, complaining about Power's "prima donna temperament." Eventually, Creel was called in to mediate. When he sided with Fosdick, Powers had yet another reason to be dissatisfied with the CPI.[36]

Powers had the perfect means to amplify his charges before the Ways and Means Committee—*The Yanks Are Coming,* a film Universal had shot at the Dayton-Wright airplane factory. When Universal officials announced that *The Yanks Are Coming* would be shown at the Broadway Theater in New York City on June 23, 1918, they were fully aware that government agents would seize the film, since Universal had not secured the required CPI shooting permits. On the night of the film's premiere, a sign was hung in the lobby which read: "*The Yanks Are Coming,* advertised to be Tonight, Stopped by the Creel-Hearst Committee."[37] The theater was completely sold out when Universal's attorney, James M. Sheen, walked dramatically in front of the screen and repeated Power's contention that the film could not be shown because of Hearst influence within the CPI.[38] The next day, under the headline, "War Film Stopped; Hearst Influence on Creel Blamed," the *New York Times* gave Universal's charges front-page coverage. Universal's Robert H. Cochrane held a press conference where he passed out a list of twelve Hearst-CPI employees who were supposedly responsible for blocking *The Yanks Are Coming.*[39]

Universal's attack placed the CPI on the defensive. Hart held his own press conference, where he contended that no one on the CPI payroll was still a Hearst employee, and that none of the so-called "Hearstlings" were in a position to influence the Committee's decision about *The Yanks Are Coming.* With a total of sixty-one employees in the CPI film division, Hart concluded that there was nothing unusual about a few staff members having been employed by the huge Hearst organization.[40]

On June 25, 1918, George Creel provided the press with an official statement of the CPI's position in the Universal affair:

> The motion picture, *The Yanks Are Coming,* was refused the necessary official sanctions because every detail of the film's making was in open disregard and even defiance of established procedure. No photographs may be made in any factory doing Government work without formal permits, issued after investigation. Universal did not have these permits, and made no effort to get them. Also, after making the pictures without permits,

Universal planned a commercial exploitation of the film for its own profit, a privilege denied every other motion picture producer in the United States at one time or another.

The only question in issue is whether private greed shall have the power to nullify the Government's efforts to protect military secrets. The charge of Hearst influence is merely an attempt to muddy the water, and is as absurd as it is indecent. No one in connection with this organization had responsibility in the matter save myself. The decision was my own and others merely carried out my explicit instructions.[41]

The War Department backed Creel's position with a supportive statement from Secretary of War Baker, and appointed Major Nicholas Biddle, chief of the Army Intelligence Service in New York, to mediate the conflict between the CPI and Universal.[42] Although *The Yanks Are Coming* was never publicly released, the War Department eventually showed the film to Dayton-Wright employees and donated a print of the film to the Bureau of Aircraft Production in Washington.[43]

The primary result of these charges and countercharges was renewed Congressional scrutiny. Representative Allen T. Treadway of Massachusetts, a frequent critic of the CPI, called for a complete investigation of the CPI's motion picture program. Treadway also introduced a resolution asking Secretary Baker to provide the Military Affairs Committee with a report to explain the agreements between the Signal Corps, the CPI, and the private film industry.[44]

Creel probably felt that he had answered most of these questions in his earlier appearance before the House Appropriations Committee, but after reports surfaced that he was opposed to Treadway's investigation, he appeared at the Military Affairs Committee's hearings.[45] Creel outlined the CPI's negotiations over the *Official War Review*, explaining that Pathe had made the highest bid and that it was returning 80 percent of the profits to the government, a fact which belied Universal's charges that Pathe was receiving special treatment. Creel also pointed out that Universal, like any other newsreel company, could purchase war films not used in the *Official War Review* for the nominal charge of one dollar per foot.[46]

Creel also helped Secretary Baker draft his response to the Treadway resolution. Baker's report to the Military Affairs Committee pointed out that all of the Allied film services sold their films in the commercial marketplace and that the House Appropriations Committee had, in effect, agreed that the CPI could do the same thing. Although Baker did not mention Universal by name, he also noted that the American film industry "with one exception, understands this arrangement, acquiesces to it, and is giving the Committee On Public Information whole-hearted support. . . ."[47]

The controversy generated by the Universal affair began to dissipate a short time after the Military Affairs hearings closed. Universal never presented convincing evidence of Hearst influence and most people evidently accepted the CPI's explanation. For nearly a month the Division of Films had been subjected to a searching examination in Congress and the press. If anything, the Division of Films emerged from these investigations in a stronger position. The House, however begrudgingly, granted the CPI the right to sell government-financed films in the commercial marketplace. Furthermore, the private film industry, with the exception of Universal, still seemed more than willing to provide the government with its crucial support.

The film industry's passive attitude is all the more striking because of its prewar campaign against government censorship and regulation. The industry's one real protest had actually grown out of personality conflicts and supposed business advantages—not First Amendment issues. Again, the overwhelming desire to obtain official recognition and approval seemed to paralyze the film industry. Perhaps, if the war had continued longer, the industry would have mobilized its forces against government censorship and export regulations. In the closing days of the war, however, these issues paled beside the threat of new government regulations.

## The Essential Industry

From the film industry's point of view, it had done everything the government wanted, and more. The industry's official War Cooperation Committee had produced thousands of slides, trailers, and promotional films for the government. Movie stars had sold war bonds, encouraged enlistment, and explained conservation programs. Theater owners had displayed government posters in their lobbies, and allowed the CPI's Four-Minute Men to speak, supposedly for four minutes, between reel changes in their film programs. The industry had submitted, without a whimper, to government permit systems, informal censorship, and export regulations. And if that was not enough, the industry had allowed government-financed films to be distributed and exhibited through its regular commercial channels—and then paid for the privilege of doing so. Yet even with its good service record, the industry discovered that different government agencies were planning still newer government programs that could close movie theaters, or, in the worst case, shut down the entire film business.

The first new program was a brainstorm from Harry Garfield's Fuel Adminstration. As a means of conserving coal and electricity, the Fuel Administration ordered movie theaters closed each Tuesday of the week. The expected industry protest quickly dissipated when it was learned that Garfield's agency had initially considered closing the theaters three days each week.[48]

The industry's greatest threat, however, came from the War Industries Board, headed by Bernard M. Baruch. President Wilson created the War

Figure 54. Speakers from the CPI's Four-Minute Men organization pose for a 1918 photograph in New York. (War Department Photo. National Archives)

Industries Board fairly late in the war, April 6, 1918, as a means of coordinating the nation's industries and resources, eliminating waste, and insuring the military of necessary supplies. If the Board ruled that motion pictures were "non-essential," a possibility given the movies' entertainment orientation, the film industry would have effectively been put out of business for the remainder of the First World War.[49]

Film companies had already been hit hard at the box office during the spring of 1918 due to a serious flu epidemic and public confusion about the Fuel Administration's energy conservation program. With the War Industries Board seemingly ready to sound the death knell, William Brady sent a telegram to George Creel, complaining bitterly about the "hysterical patriotic wave sweeping over the country that it was unpatriotic to attend moving pictures during the war on the ground that moving pictures are classified as non-essentials. . . ." To underscore the seriousness of the problem, Brady revealed that one-third of the movie theaters in Los Angeles had already closed. He begged Creel to contact other government officials as a means of obtaining some kind of relief for the film industry.[50]

Creel immediately sent telegrams to Treasury Secretary William McAdoo, Herbert Hoover of the Food Administration, and Harry Garfield of the Fuel Administration, asking them to comment on the movies' importance. "As you know," Creel added, "the fifty thousand Four Minute Men use the motion picture theatres, the film plays a big part in every one of our drives, and . . . constitutes one of our most effective aids in the matter of publicity."[51]

Each of these officials responded positively to Creel's request and their letters were later published in an elaborate brief prepared by the National Association of the Motion Picture Industry. It presented virtually every shred of evidence the industry possessed regarding what the NAMPI described as the "reasons, facts, arguments for declaring the motion picture industry an essential industry." The brief contained Wilson's letter asking Brady to form the industry's War Cooperation Committee, letters of praise from Creel and Charles Hart, and a detailed outline of the many services the industry had performed for the CPI, Treasury Department, Army, Navy, Red Cross, Y.M.C.A., and the Food and Fuel Administrations.[52]

Brady also sent a telegram to Wilson's secretary Tumulty, asking him to use his "personal influence in any way which will tend to secure a withdrawal . . . of an order which would classify the motion picture industry as non-essential."[53] There is no record of Wilson's response, but after a meeting between the War Industries Board and officials of the NAMPI, chairman Baruch declared the motion picture an "essential industry" on August 23, 1918.[54]

The film industry was overjoyed, viewing the Board's declaration not only as a sign of approval for the industry's war work, but as the culmination

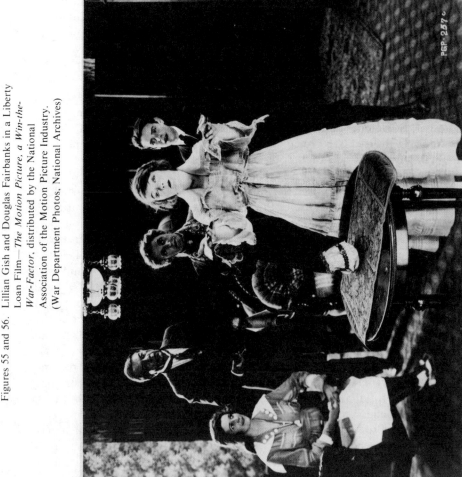

Figures 55 and 56. Lillian Gish and Douglas Fairbanks in a Liberty Loan Film—*The Motion Picture, a Win-the-War-Factor*, distributed by the National Association of the Motion Picture Industry. (War Department Photos, National Archives)

of the industry's lifelong quest for recognition and respect. In a few short years, the American film industry had matured into a major communications medium, a medium officially recognized by the United States government as essential to the life of the nation.[55]

Near the end of 1918 one of the new motion picture trade magazines, *Wid's Year Book,* asked a number of leading film producers and directors what they considered "the most important happening" in the American film industry during the preceding year.[56] This admittedly unscientific survey gave most of the filmmakers an opportunity to comment on the exciting new role the motion pictures played during the First World War. Cecil B. DeMille, a young director for the Famous Players Company, described the movies' special power to make a viewer vicariously experience the "world-drama going on over there." D. W. Griffith, fresh from directing war pictures at the request of the French and British governments, praised the British War Office for selecting the motion picture as "the major medium for propaganda, educational, and publicity work." Director Maurice Tourneur pointed to the government's decision to recognize the American motion picture business as an essential wartime industry. But it was left to Adolph Zukor, the head of filmdom's largest and most powerful company, Paramount Pictures, to explain what "essential-industry" status really meant to the American film industry:

> Long before this year, the world accepted the motion picture as the foremost agency of entertainment and amusement extant; but it remained for the activities of the past year to register indisputably the fact that as an avenue of propaganda, as a channel for conveying thought and opinion the movies are unequalled by any form of communication. . . .
>
> In a greater measure than ever before in its entire history, the cultivated and cultured people of the country have found in the motion picture a genuine appeal to their minds and hearts. The motion picture is therefore no longer the theatre of the masses, but is today the amusement of the masses and classes. College professors, authors, lecturers, men of all professional and scholastic fields have found in the photoplay as deep and vital a lore as they have found in the product of the pulpit, the platform and the library. The motion picture has found its place in the intellectual sun, and its power to kindle the spirits and touch the imagination is now adorned with a new psychic ability to reach the soul and heart of mankind.[57]

Perhaps all of these filmmakers were simply swept away on a wave of wartime patriotism. Yet the industry's war work and the U.S. government's full-scale motion picture program argued otherwise. What Zukor described as the movie's place in the sun had nothing to do with California. The motion picture had come of age socially and politically.

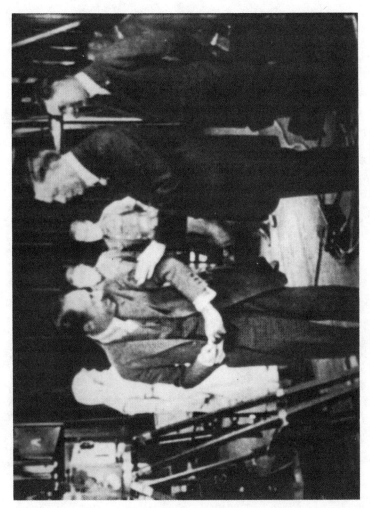

Figure 57.   Contemporary newsreel showing D. W. Griffith as he
receives a badge for his participation in the War Savings
Stamp program.
(Post-Newsweek Television Stations, Inc. and Blackhawk
Films)

# Epilogue

At hearings before the House Appropriations Committee in the summer of 1918, Dr. Guy Stanton Ford, professor of European history, dean of the Graduate School at the University of Minnesota, and head of the CPI's Division of Civic and Educational Cooperation, provided an assessment of George Creel and the United States government's World War I film campaign:

> A man who had worked in the government in the ordinary way would have said at once, "The government cannot go into the motion-picture business." But here was a man who saw what others had not seen clearly enough in the past, that such a thing has infinite possibilities for good if it is organized in the right way, and that you can teach through the eyes and through these pictures what neither the printed nor the spoken word can teach. He caught the idea and he pushed it; and its possibilities as an instrument in patriotic education are evident.[1]

In the wake of the government's wartime motion picture effort, such optimism about the "possibilities" of government filmmaking is understandable. Yet the development of a U.S. government film program was by no means a certainty when the First World War began. The Committee on Public Information had neither a plan of action nor a feasibility study waiting on the shelf to guide its efforts to use motion pictures as a channel for public information and persuasion. With almost no prior preparation and with limited filmmaking experience, the U.S. government's World War I film program grew as much out of accident and circumstance as careful planning.

The Army Signal Corps' decision to produce a "pictorial history" of the Great War provided much of the impetus for the creation of a Film Division within the CPI. At first, the Division of Films limited itself to free distribution of Signal Corps films, but the appointment of Charles Hart as division chairman in early 1918 signaled a rapid expansion of government film activity. By the end of the war the CPI's Division of Films had developed the capability of making, distributing and exhibiting films. The CPI Scenario

Department might have plunged the government even more deeply into the movie business had the war not ended so quickly. Instead of writing scripts to be shot by commercial producers, the Scenario Department wrote, shot and edited its own films. Commercial filmmakers were no longer needed.

Most of the CPI's films, of course, were produced too late in the war to have the kind of impact on public opinion which the CPI later claimed for its film effort. Still, films made by the Division of Films were seen throughout the United States and in many foreign countries. With the all-important assistance of the private film industry, motion pictures were used to sell war bonds, encourage enlistment, and to explain the need for conserving food and fuel. Motion picture stars traveled throughout the country, promoting patriotism and securing subscriptions for the government's Liberty Loan drives. With their ready-made audiences, motion picture theaters provided the ideal forum for government sponsored speechmakers. Representative Charles B. Smith of New York was so impressed with the potential of screen publicity that he introduced a resolution in the House asking the secretary of commerce to study the possibility of using motion pictures to promote interstate and foreign commerce.[2]

Such hopes were a natural outgrowth of the government's film effort. But the signing of the armistice did not herald a golden age of government filmmaking. Once the war ended and the CPI was disbanded, the private film industry's interest in government filmmaking vanished as quickly as it had started after the American declaration of war. Not until the 1930s and the work of Pare Lorentz and the short-lived United States Film Service did government films appear with any regularity in commercial movie theaters. Nevertheless, the the work of the Army Signal Corps and the CPI Division of Films provided countless precedents for the film programs of the Office of War Information and the Signal Corps Photographic Center in World War II. For better or worse, virtually every technique for producing, distributing or exhibiting government films had already been tried and tested by the Committee on Public Information in the First World War.

In many respects, Charles Hart's greatest success was not in making government films but in getting them seen. Without the help of the American film industry this would not have been possible. The industry's trade associations, war cooperation committees and its stars provided invaluable support for a number of the government's wartime publicity campaigns, but the industry's most important contribution was giving the CPI access to its movie screens. If the CPI's newsreels and feature films had not been shown in commercial movie theaters, most Americans would simply never have seen them, and the CPI's film program would have been deprived of the income it so desperately needed to expand its work at home and abroad.

Figures 58 and 59.  Japanese-American actor Sessue Hayakawa in a
Liberty Loan film production and as bond
salesman at a Liberty Loan rally.
(Post-Newsweek Television Stations, Inc. and
Blackhawk Films)

Through the enormous war powers of agencies such as the Fuel Administration and the War Trade Board, the government possessed the means to force the industry's cooperation. Yet there is little evidence that the government had to resort to pressure to gain the industry's assistance. If anything, the government actually had to fight off industry volunteers, sifting through an endless stream of motion picture publicity schemes and would-be government filmmakers. This overwhelming support is all the more striking in light of the film industry's prewar fear of government regulation and censorship. Although the CPI possessed no statutory authority to regulate screen content, a series of regulations and executive orders enabled the CPI to put considerable pressure on filmmakers to alter the content of films it found objectionable. Through its use of War Trade Board export regulations, the CPI exerted even greater control over the content of American motion pictures that went abroad. It is likely, of course, that the CPI's foreign film campaign actually helped the American film industry, particularly in its efforts to drive German films off the neutral screens of Europe. The government also aggressively pushed American films into new foreign markets as a means of expanding the CPI's propaganda campaign, an effort with obvious benefits for the American film industry. By the end of the war, the industry completely dominated world film trade. This is an area, certainly, which warrants further investigation.

In the end, the attempt to use motion pictures as a persuasive weapon in World War I was far more important to the American film industry than to the United States government. It is important to note that the Great War occurred at a point in film history when the motion picture was evolving into a major form of mass entertainment and communication. Many of the changes were not war-related: the introduction of feature-length films, the development of the star system, and the construction of spectacular "movie palaces." By the end of the war, however, the American film industry had achieved a goal which had obsessed industry leaders from the movies' inception—official recognition for the motion picture medium. Through participation in the U.S. government's World War I film program and increased contact with government officials, the American film industry obtained a degree of respectability and acceptance unimaginable prior to the Great War.

Filmmakers corresponded regularly with the president; actor Douglas Fairbanks gave him a movie projector which was installed in the White House.[3] After the war, a number of Treasury Department officials who had worked closely with the industry during the Liberty Loan campaigns actually went into the film business. Treasury Secretary William McAdoo, Wilson's son-in-law, was offered the presidency of the new United Artists Corporation, a company formed by the stars of the loan drives: Charlie Chaplin, Mary

Figure 60.   George Creel and President Woodrow Wilson together
on a Swiss train platform after the war.
(War Department Photo, National Archives)

Pickford, D. W. Griffith and Douglas Fairbanks. McAdoo declined this offer, but did agree to serve as the counsel for United Artists. McAdoo's first assistant at Treasury, Oscar Price, was appointed to United Artists' board of directors, and the Treasury's chief publicity engineer, Frank Wilson, later formed a motion picture finance company and produced educational films.[4]

The first issue of the *Fox News,* later to become the largest and most powerful American screen magazine—*The Fox Movietone Newsreel*—was released on October 3, 1919: It opens dramatically with a blank sheet of paper. Slowly, a hand enters from the side of the frame and begins rubbing a coin across the blank page. As if by magic, the following words appear:

> I am very much interested and deeply gratified to learn that the Fox Film Company is intending to devote its news weekly to the promotion of universal and lasting peace. It can render the greatest service in this direction. The Moving Picture News Weekly as an educator and a power for good can be made of the greatest service to the nation and to observant people everywhere throughout the world, and I congratulate the company upon its public-spirited plan.
>
> Cordially and sincerely,
> Woodrow Wilson[5]

Prior to World War I and the United States government's official film effort, such a letter would have been highly unusual and the cause of considerable rejoicing in the American film industry. But by the end of the war, such an endorsement from the president of the United States was almost commonplace, common enough, at least, that the filmmakers felt some need to embellish its presentation on the screen. From the day only a few years earlier when Universal's president Carl Laemmle tried to arrange a meeting with President Woodrow Wilson so that he could simply shake hands, the movie men and the motion pictures had come a long, long way.

# Notes

## Chapter 1

1. See Richard D. MacCann, *The People's Film: A Political History of U.S. Government Motion Pictures* (New York: Hastings House, 1973), pp. 43–44; and Raymond Evans, "USDA Motion Picture Service 1908–1943," *Business Screen*, V, No. 1 (1943), p. 20.

2. George Creel, *How We Advertised America: The First Telling of the Amazing Story of the Committee on Public Information That Carried the Gospel of Americanism to Every Corner of the Globe* (New York: Harper and Bros., 1920), pp. 117–125. For a brief overview of Signal Corps film activities in World War I see K. Jack Bauer, comp., "List of World War I Signal Corps Films," Special Lists No. 14, National Archives and Records Service (Washington: 1957), pp. 1–2.

3. See especially Robert C. Hilderbrand, "Power and the People: Executive Management of Public Opinion in Foreign Affairs, 1859–1921" (unpublished Ph.D. dissertation, University of Iowa, 1977), pp. 505–509. Hilderbrand, incidentally, credits President William McKinley rather than Theodore Roosevelt as the originator of skillful executive publicity.

   For a study which examines the impact of progressive ideology on the CPI, see Stephen Vaughn, *Holding Fast the Inner Lines: Democracy, Nationalism, and the Committee on Public Information* (Chapel Hill: University of North Carolina Press, 1980), pp. 23–28.

4. Among the many studies devoted to the development of the American film industry in this period are: Terry Ramsaye, *A Million and One Nights* (New York: Simon and Schuster, 1926); Lewis Jacobs, *The Rise of the American Film* (New York: Teacher's College Press, 1938); Garth Jowett, *Film: The Democratic Art* (Boston: Little, Brown and Co., 1976); Benjamin B. Hampton, *A History of the American Film Industry: From Its Beginnings to 1931* (1931; rev. ed. New York: Dover Publications, 1970); Mae D. Heuttig, *Economic Control of the Motion Picture Industry: A Study in Industrial Organization* (Philadelphia: University of Pennsylvania Press, 1944).

5. Heuttig, pp. 30–31. See also William M. Seabury, *The Public and the Motion Picture Industry* (New York: The Macmillan Company, 1926), p. 18. Another excellent study of the economic development of the early motion picture industry is found in Howard T. Lewis, *The Motion Picture Industry* (New York: D. Van Nostrand Company, 1933).

6. Jacobs, p. 108.

7. Ibid., p. 159.

8. Hampton, p. 66.

9. The motion picture trade papers were filled with accounts of the war's impact on European film companies. See "The War and Pictures," *Moving Picture World,* August 15, 1914, pp. 963–964; "Pathe Discontinues Daily," *Moving Picture World,* August 15, 1914, p. 1972; "The European War," *Moving Picture World,* September 5, 1914, p. 1343; Henry C. Dodge, "The Movies of War-Time Paris," *Photoplay,* June 1916, pp. 70–74.

10. "Trade Notes," *Moving Picture World,* September 5, 1914, p. 1343.

11. "British Notes," *Moving Picture World,* May 1, 1915, p. 1263.

12. "Big Jump in Film Exports," *Moving Picture World,* November 20, 1915, p. 1518.

13. Cal York, "Plays and Players," *Photoplay,* May 1917, p. 63. See also Cal York, "Must Have Their Movies," *Photoplay,* July, 1917, p. 153.

14. W. Stephen Bush, "Here is Cine-Mundial," *Moving Picture World,* December 18, 1915, pp. 2154–2155.

15. Ibid.; see also F. G. Orteyga, "Random Shots About Export," *Moving Picture World,* March 10, 1917, p. 1515.

16. Advertisement, *Moving Picture World,* December 16, 1916, p. 1585. By the end of 1915, Fox and three other companies (Metro, World and Paramount) had acquired distributing organizations in Canada as well. See "Latest American Company in Canada," *Moving Picture World,* December 18, 1915, p. 2228.

17. "American Film Invasion of Brazil," *Moving Picture World,* December 30, 1916, p. 1936.

18. See Jacob Binder to Joseph P. Tumulty, January 24, 1916, Series 4, File 72, Woodrow Wilson Papers (Library of Congress Microfilm), Reel 283. All citations hereafter will simply cite Wilson Papers and the microfilm reel number.

19. Raymond A. Cook, *Thomas Dixon,* ed. Sylvia E. Bowman, *Twayne's United States Authors Series,* Vol. 235 (New York: Twayne Publishers, 1965), p. 115.

20. This statement is quoted in many studies which deal with *The Birth of a Nation,* including Milton Mackaye, "The Birth of a Nation," *Scribner's Magazine,* CII, No. 5 (November, 1937), p. 69; Jacobs, *Rise of American Film,* p. 175; Russell Merritt, "Dixon, Griffith and the Southern Legend," *Cinema Journal,* XII, No. 1 (Fall, 1972), p. 18; Thomas R. Cripps, "The Reaction of the Negro to *The Birth of a Nation,*" *The Historian,* XXV, No. 3 (May, 1963), p. 349; and Cook, p. 115.

21. Cripps, p. 359.

22. Thomas Dixon to Woodrow Wilson, March 5, 1915, Ser. 4, File 2247, Wilson Papers, Reel 332. Both Arthur S. Link, *Wilson: The New Freedom, 1912–1914* (Princeton: Princeton University Press, 1956), pp. 252–253, and Cripps, pp. 348–349, suggest that Dixon arranged the White House screening primarily to head off criticism about the film.

23. E. D. White to Tumulty, April 5, 1915, Ser. 4, File 76A, Wilson Papers, Reel 199. For an account of the hearings see Mrs. Walter M. Damrosch to Tumulty, March 27, 1915, Ser. 4, File 2247, Wilson Papers, Reel 332.

24. Tumulty to Thomas C. Thatcher, April 28, 1915, Ser. 4, File 72, Wilson Papers, Reel 198; Thatcher to Tumulty, April 17, 1915, Ser. 4, File 2247, Wilson Papers, Reel 332.

25. D. W. Griffith to Wilson, March 2, 1915, Ser. 2, File March 2–April 12, Wilson Papers, Reel 69.

26. Wilson to Griffith, March 5, 1915, Ser. 4, File 72, Wilson Papers, Reel 198. In 1916, Griffith sought Wilson's opinion about a proposed film on George Washington. Wilson expressed interest in the project, but suggested that Griffith discuss the project with Colonel House. See Griffith to Wilson, May 4, 1916; Memorandum, Tumulty to Wilson, May 11, 1916, and attached note, Wilson to Tumulty, undated but May, 1916; all in Ser. 4, File 72, Wilson Papers, Reel 198.

27. Robert Sklar, *Movie-Made America: A Cultural History of American Movies* (New York: Random House, 1976), p. vi.

28. Will Irwin, *The House That Shadows Built* (Garden City: Doubleday and Company, 1928), p. 151.

29. Hal Reid to Tumulty, April 22, 1915, Ser. 4, File 72, Wilson Papers, Reel 199. Many filmmakers contacted the president during the war with ideas for using motion pictures. See, for example, Walter A. Fairservis to Tumulty, July 26, 1915, Ser. 4, File 72, Wilson Papers, Reel 198; John H. Blackmore to Tumulty, April 13, 1916; Hal Reid to Tumulty, October 9, 1916; all in Ser. 4, File 72, Wilson Papers, Reel 199.

30. *War Revenue Bill,* Statutes at Large, Vol. 38, Pt. I, 745 (1914).

31. Richard S. Randall, *Censorship of the Movies: The Social and Political Control of a Mass Medium* (Madison: The University of Wisconsin Press, 1968), pp. 3–13.

32. Jowett, *The Democratic Art,* pp. 122–123; For the bill itself and some supporting arguments see William S. Chase, pamphlet published by the Society for the Prevention of Crime, February 8, 1915, Ser. 4, File 72A, Wilson Papers, Reel 199.

33. Quoted in W. Stephen Bush, "The Motion Picture Board of Trade," *Moving Picture World,* September 25, 1915, p. 2156. See also "Film Men Form Board of Trade," *New York Times,* August 6, 1915, p. 6, c. 2; and "Observations," *Moving Picture World,* September 25, 1915, p. 2193.

34. Jacob W. Binder to Wilson, December 10, 1915, Ser. 4, File 501C, Wilson Papers, Reel 283.

35. Binder to Tumulty, December 10, 1915, Ser. 4, File 501C, Wilson Papers, Reel 283.

36. Ibid.

37. Ibid. For later industry attempts to draw the president out on the censorship question see William A. Brady to Wilson, September 13, 1916 and Binder, February 17, 1916, both in Ser. 4, File 72A, Wilson Papers, Reel 199.

38. Quoted in "President Tells of Humbugs at Large," *New York Times,* January 28, 1916, p. 2, c. 4. See also "Prepare, President Wilson Pleads," *New York Times,* January 28, 1916, p. 1, c. 1.

39. W. Stephen Bush, "Right the War Tax," *Moving Picture World,* November 20, 1915, p. 1454. See also "Brady Denounces Motion Picture Tax," *New York Times,* July 16, 1916, Sec. I, p. 14, c. 3; "Denounces Foes of Film," *New York Times,* July 14, 1916, p. 9, c. 8; Clarence L. Linz, "Congress Passes Federal Tax Bill," *Moving Picture World,* September 23, 1916, p. 1949; Clarence L. Linz, "Picture Men Urge Substitute War Tax," *Moving Picture World,* May 26, 1917, p. 1267.

40. See, for example, Hal Reid to Tumulty, March 4, 1913; Reid to Tumulty, March 7, 1913; Reid to Tumulty, April 4, 1913; Frank Dart to Wilson, November 17, 1913; all in Ser. 4, File 72, Wilson Papers, Reel 198.

One enterprising cameraman, H. A. Spaweth, tried to convince Wilson to appoint him "the official government motion picture photographer." See Spaweth to Wilson, March 28, 1913; and Spaweth to Wilson, April 1, 1913; both in Ser. 4, File 72, Wilson Papers, Reel 198.

41. Carl Laemmle to Wilson, March 5, 1915, Ser. 3, Vol. 21, Wilson Papers, Reel 141.

42. Wilson to Laemmle, December 29, 1915, Ser. 4, File 72, Wilson Papers, Reel 199.

43. Telegram, Laemmle to Wilson, December 30, 1915, Ser. 4, File 72, Wilson Papers, Reel 199.

44. Telegram, Wilson to Laemmle, December 30, 1915, Ser. 4, File 72, Wilson Papers, Reel 199. See also "Greetings on Film," *New York Times,* December 31, 1915, p. 6, c. 1. Other respondents included Postmaster General Albert S. Burleson; Secretary of the Interior Frank L. Lane; Secretary of Commerce William C. Redfield; Secretary of the Treasury (and Wilson's son-in-law) William G. McAdoo; Secretary of the Navy Josephus Daniels; and William Jennings Bryan.

45. Edward L. Fox to Tumulty, March 4, 1916, Ser. 4, File 72, Wilson Papers, Reel 199.

46. Memorandum, Wilson to Tumulty, undated but attached to Fox to Tumulty, March 4, 1916, Ser. 4, File 72, Wilson Papers, Reel 199.

47. Memorandum, Wilson to Tumulty, June 16, 1916, Ser. 4, File 72, Wilson Papers, Reel 199.

48. One example of Brady's political interest is a list of "prominent theatrical people" which he sent to Wilson with the assurance that they could be "made to see the light" in the upcoming election campaign. Among others, this list included the names of George M. Cohan, Pat A. Powers of Universal, Adolph Zukor and Jules Brulator. See Brady to Tumulty, August 31, 1916, Ser. 4, File 3249, Wilson Papers, Reel 346.

49. Brady to Tumulty, July 31, 1916, Ser. 4, File 72, Wilson Papers, Reel 199.

50. Memorandum, Wilson to Tumulty, undated but April, 1916, Ser. 4, File 72, Wilson Papers, Reel 199.

51. Memorandum, Wilson to Tumulty, undated but late August, 1916, Ser. 4, File 72, Wilson Papers, Reel 199.

52. S. A. Bloch to Tumulty, July 6, 1916, Ser. 4, File 72, Wilson Papers, Reel 199. For a similar "talking picture" scheme see F. B. Lynch to Tumulty, May 13, 1916, Ser. 4, File 72, Wilson Papers, Reel 199.

53. C. William Woodrop, the vice-president of the Columbia Gramophone Company, to Wilson, May 15, 1917; Memorandum, Wilson to Tumulty, May 15, 1917; both in Ser. 4, File 3341, Wilson Papers, Reel 348. Referring to his previous attempt at recording speeches, Wilson told Tumulty that " . . . it did not sound like my voice and was stiff as starch." See Memorandum, Wilson to Tumulty, August 10, 1916, Ser. 4, File 72, Wilson Papers, Reel 199.

54. Jacobs, *Rise of the American Film,* p. 250. *Civilization* was also known as *He Who Returned.* There is a viewing print in the Library of Congress/American Film Institute Collection.

55. Ramsaye, *A Million and One Nights,* p. 728.

56. Wilson to Thomas Ince, November 3, 1916; Wilson to Ince, October 30, 1916; both in Ser. 3, Vol. 33, Wilson Papers, Reel 147.

57.  Alec Lorimotz to Wilson, April 10, 1916; and John H. Blackwood to Tumulty, April 10, 1916; both in Ser. 4, File 72, Wilson Papers, Reel 199.

58.  "Hughes and T. R. in Movies," *New York Times*, August 26, 1916, p. 4, c. 3. Hal Reid also tried to persuade Wilson to let him make a campaign film for the Democratic Party. See Reid to Wilson, April 18, 1916, Ser. 4, File 72, Wilson Papers, Reel 199.

59.  C. R. Macauley to Tumulty, October 3, 1916, Ser. 4, File 80, Wilson Papers, Reel 200; Edward L. Fox to Tumulty, April 20, 1916; and E. Cohn of the Pathe Newsreel Company to Tumulty, August 26, 1916; both in Ser. 4, File 72, Wilson Papers, Reel 199.

**Chapter 2**

1.  Quoted in Ray Stannard Baker, *Woodrow Wilson, Life and Letters,* V (Garden City: Doubleday and Company, 1935), p. 18. For an excellent analysis of the neutrality period see Arthur S. Link, *Woodrow Wilson and the Progressive Era, 1910–1917* (New York: Harper Torchbooks, 1963), especially Chapter 8, "Devious Diplomacy," pp. 197–222; also John Patrick Finnegan, *Against the Specter of a Dragon: The Campaign for American Military Preparedness, 1914–1917* (Boston: Houghton Mifflin, 1935).

2.  Raymond Fielding, *The American Newsreel, 1911–1967* (Norman: University of Oklahoma Press, 1972), pp. 70–76.

3.  Advertisements, *Moving Picture World*, August 15, 1914, pp. 196–197 and p. 1005. Also August 22, 1914, pp. 1059–1061.

4.  Jacobs, *Rise of American Film*, p. 12.

5.  Jowett, *The Democratic Art*, p. 38. He feels that the movies may have "acted as a guide to the newcomer on the manners and customs of his new environment." See also John Higham, *Strangers in the Land: Patterns of American Nativism* (New York: Atheneum, 1963), pp. 191–198.

6.  "Fake War Pictures Stir East Side," *New York Times*, September 6, 1915, p. 6, c. 1. See also W. Stephen Bush, "War Films," *Moving Picture World*, September 19, 1914, p. 1617.
    There were very few cases in which a film was censored on political grounds during the neutrality years. In September of 1915, Henrich Charles, secretary of the Chamber of German-American Commerce, appealed to the National Board of Censorship to ban *The Ordeal*, a film by the Life Photo Film Company which allegedly showed German atrocities in Belgium. Calling the film "a flagrant violation of President Wilson's injunction of neutrality," Charles urged the Board to revoke the film's license. See "Move to Suppress Belgian Pictures," *New York Times*, September 16, 1914, p. 4, c. 7. For a time *The Ordeal* was actually withdrawn by the New York Commissioner of Licenses, who feared that the film might stir up anti-German sentiments, but in the wake of the *Lusitania* crisis, the New York Supreme Court lifted the ban on the film in May of 1915. See "Court Lifts the Hyphen out of Citizenship," *New York Times*, May 27, 1915, p. 5, c. 7; "Ban Lifted on *Ordeal*," *Moving Picture World*, June 12, 1915, p. 1731. For a review of the film see "The Ordeal," *Moving Picture World*, November 14, 1914, p. 934.

7.  "Fake War Pictures Stir East Side," *New York Times*, September 6, 1914, p. 6, c. 1.

8.  "Warn Motion Picture Men," *New York Times*, August 24, 1914, p. 9, c. 2. See also J. W. Binder to Wilson, August 27, 1914, Ser. 4, File 72, Wilson Papers, Reel 198.

9. William Jennings Bryan to Wilson, August 10, 1914, Ser. 4, File 72, Wilson Papers, Reel 198. After the sinking of the Lusitania in 1915, film exhibitors in Philadelphia agreed to refrain from showing scenes of the European war, a move heartily endorsed by Mayor Rudolph Blankenburg. "Neutrality at Shows," *Moving Picture World,* June 5, 1915, p. 1164. See also W. Stephen Bush, "The Exhibitor's Power," *Moving Picture World,* June 19, 1915, p. 1913. Commenting on "hyphenated citizens" who wanted to take sides in the movie theater, Bush suggests that their place "is in the trenches where no doubt any one of the belligerent nations will be glad to have them."

10. Paul Gulick to Wilson, September 8, 1914, Ser. 4, File 72, Wilson Papers, Reel 198. See also Jack Cohn to Tumulty, October 30, 1914, Ser. 4, File 72, Wilson Papers, Reel 198.

11. Review, "Be Neutral," *Moving Picture World,* September 18, 1914, p. 1650.

12. Jack Cohn to Tumulty, October 20, 1914, Ser. 4, File 72, Wilson Papers, Reel 198.

13. "Advance Notes," *Moving Picture World,* August 15, 1914, p. 873.

14. Judson C. Hanford, "European Armies in Action," *Moving Picture World,* August 22, 1914, p. 1079. See also "Calendar of Licensed Releases," *Moving Picture World,* August 8, 1914, p. 887.

15. One of the best accounts of World War I news filming, with a particular emphasis on the many problems faced by the hardy World War I newsreel cameramen comes from David H. Mould, *American Newsfilm, 1914–1919: The Underexposed War* (New York: Garland Publishing: Dissertations on Film, 1983). See also, Fielding, *American Newsreels,* p. 72–74.

16. J. D. Tippet, "All War Pictures Fake," *Moving Picture World,* October 3, 1914, p. 50.

17. "Fake War Movies," *Literary Digest,* November 13, 1915, p. 2375. See also Robert J. Shores, "The European War in Grantwood, New Jersey," *Motion Picture Magazine,* January, 1915, pp. 68–78.

18. "Donald Thompson's Famous War Pictures," *Moving Picture World,* February 6, 1915, p. 812. See also Mould, *American Newsfilm,* pp. 79–82.

19. Mould, p. 113.

20. Ramsaye, *A Million and One Nights,* pp. 684–685.

21. Powell is quoted in "Donald C. Thompson—Home From the Front," *Moving Picture World,* December 25, 1915, p. 2375.

22. Ernest A. Dench, "Preserving the Great War for Posterity by the Movies," *Motion Picture Magazine,* July, 1915, p. 92. See also, "On Belgian Battlefields," *Moving Picture World,* December 12, 1914, p. 1507.

23. Jasper McQuade, "Chicago Newsletter," *Moving Picture World,* January 9, 1915, p. 203.

24. Quoted in "Donald Thompson's Famous War Pictures," *Moving Picture World,* February 6, 1915, p. 812.

25. "Germans on the Screen," *New York Times,* September 21, 1915, p. 11, c. 2. See also "Sell Soda Tickets as Theater Tickets," *New York Times,* September 21, 1915, p. 11, c. 3.

26. U. S. Congress, Senate, Committee on the Judiciary, *Investigation of Brewing and Liquor Interests and German Propaganda ... Pursuant to S. Res. 307,* Hearings, 65th Cong., 2nd and 3rd Sess. (Washington: Government Printing Office, 1919), II, p. 1433. Cited hereafter as *IBLI.*

27. Ibid., pp. 1434–1435.

28. Review, "The Battle of Przemysl," *Moving Picture World,* August 14, 1915, p. 1175.

29. *IBLI,* pp. 1438–1442.

30. Ibid., p. 1440.

31. Ibid., pp. 1441–1443; and see also "German Propaganda Works on a Cash Basis," *New York Times,* August 16, 1915, p. 3, c. 3.

32. As quoted in "Malitz's Connection Legitimate," *Moving Picture World,* September 14, 1915, p. 1624.

33. *IBLI,* p. 1447.

34. "Miss Stewart at the Rialto," *New York Times,* January 1, 1917, p. 10, c. 2; and see review, "Germany and Its Armies of Today," *Moving Picture World,* January 13, 1917, p. 181 and *IBLI,* p. 2021.

35. *IBLI,* p. 1440.

36. "French Fighters in Films," *New York Times,* May 30, 1915, Sec. II, p. 3, c. 2. See also "France to Picture War," *New York Times,* April 14, 1915, p. 12, c. 4, and J. B. Sutcliffe, "British Notes," *Moving Picture World,* June 12, 1915, p. 1781.

37. "Movies Will Boost Latest French Loan," *New York Times,* November 25, 1915, p. 2, c. 5. See also "Plays and Players," *Photoplay,* November, 1915, p. 94.

38. William Gladdish, "Sunday Shows in Toronto," *Moving Picture World,* November 13, 1915, p. 1335.

39. Review, "Our American Boys in the European War," *Moving Picture World,* July 22, 1916, p. 648. See also "Ambulance Corps in France Filmed," *New York Times,* July 6, 1916, p. 11, c. 4.

40. William Flynn, "American Boys in France Filmed," *Moving Picture World,* September 9, 1916, p. 1172.

41. Quoted in "Roosevelt at Film of American Valor," *New York Times,* September 24, 1916, Sec. I, p. 4, c. 1.

42. "American Ambulance Pictures at Strand," *Moving Picture World,* December 23, 1916, p. 1781.

43. Kevin Brownlow, *The War, The West, and the Wilderness* (New York: Alfred Knopf, 1978), p. 47. See also "British Fleet in Movies," *New York Times,* October 19, 1915, p. 2, c. 4.

44. Fielding, *The American Newsreel,* p. 57, 69.

45. "How Britain Prepared," *New York Times,* May 30, 1916, p. 3, c. 4. See also review, "How Britain Prepared," *Moving Picture World,* March 25, 1916, p. 2025.

46. Franklin Roosevelt to Charles Urban, May 19, 1916. See also Newton D. Baker to Charles Urban, May 17, 1916; both in Ser. 4, File 80, Wilson Papers, Reel 200.

47. "Battle of Somme in Film," *New York Times,* September 30, 1916, p. 11, c. 2. See also J. B. Sutcliffe, "British Notes," *Moving Picture World,* October 7, 1916, p. 81, and Brownlow, *The War,* pp. 52–53.

48.  "Vanderbilt Backs War Relief Film," *New York Times,* January 17, 1917, p. 11, c. 3. See also "General Films War Pictures," *Moving Picture World,* December 23, 1916, p. 1781, and "Italy at War in Films," *New York Times,* June 13, 1916, p. 9, c. 3.

49.  Quoted in Lief Furhammar and Folke Isaksson, *Politics and Film* (New York: Praegar Publishers, 1971), p. 9. See also Roger Manvell and Heinrich Fraenkel, *The German Cinema* (London: J. M. Dent, 1971), pp. 8–9.

50.  Finnegan, *Against the Specter,* pp. 91–105; Link, *The Progressive Era,* pp. 177–178.

51.  Finnegan, pp. 26–27.

52.  Review, "The Nation's Peril," *Moving Picture World,* November 27, 1915, p. 1675; and pre-release announcement, *Moving Picture World,* October 21, 1916, p. 417. Pathe released a film by the same title in 1912 which told the story of a young spy who has a change of heart and turns in her spy master to the authorities. See review, "A Nation's Peril," *Moving Picture World,* June 15, 1912, p. 1013. See also "War Scenes in Lubin Feature," *Moving Picture World,* October 6, 1915, p. 1113, and review by Louis R. Harrison, "The Rights of Man," *Moving Picture World,* October 30, 1915, p. 813.

53.  In the same time period, several American film companies released preparedness films based on popular war songs. The Selig Company, for example, produced *I'm Glad My Boy Grew Up to Be a Soldier,* which was a parody of the pacifist war song, "I Didn't Raise My Boy to Be a Soldier." See review, *Moving Picture World,* November 27, 1915, p. 1751. The Pathe Company released *It's a Long, Long Way to Tipperary,* which was based on the popular British war song of the same name. See review, *Moving Picture World,* February 13, 1915, p. 961.

54.  Tom Moore to Tumulty, May 25, 1914, Ser. 4, File 72, Wilson Papers, Reel 198. Moore's letter suggests that he arranged a special screening on the White House lawn in the summer of 1914 for Wilson of the Italian feature film *Cabiria.*

55.  William H. Rudolph to Tumulty, August 5, 1915, Ser. 4, File 72, Wilson Papers, Reel 1918. See also review, "Guarding Old Glory," *Moving Picture World,* June 15, 1915, p. 1785, and positive comments from Secretary Garrison in "Secretary Praises Guarding Old Glory," *Moving Picture World,* December 25, 1915, p. 2046.

56.  Finnegan, *Against the Specter,* p. 37; Link, *The Progressive Era,* pp. 178–179.

57.  Hudson Maxim, *Defenseless America* (New York: Hearst International Library, 1916), p. 4.

58.  Anthony Slide, *The Big V: A History of the Vitagraph Company* (Metuchen, N. J.: The Scarecrow Press, 1976), p. 73. For an excellent analysis of *The Battle Cry of Peace,* see Brownlow, *The War,* pp. 30–38.

59.  Slide, pp. 75–76; and "Preparedness Pleas as a Movie Theme," *New York Times,* August 6, 1915, p. 6, c. 1.

60.  Walter A. Fairservis to Tumulty, July 26, 1915 and August 3, 1915; both in Ser. 4, File 72, Wilson Papers, Reel 198. See also, "See Big Invasion Film," *New York Times,* August 11, 1915, p. 6, c. 3. See also "New York Shelled on Movie Screen," *New York Times,* August 7, 1915, p. 8, c. 2. The *Times* reviewer said that it was "difficult to escape the impression that you are supposed to recognize the nationality. They are not Portuguese for instance."

61.  "Big Opening for Vitagraph Feature," *Moving Picture World,* September 25, 1915, p. 2158; see also Slide, pp. 77–78.

62. Jasper S. McQuade, "Chicago Newsletter," *Moving Picture World,* November 6, 1915, p. 1142; Kenneth C. Crain, "Preparedness Film Stirs," *Moving Picture World,* December 18, 1915, p. 2219.

63. Brownlow, *The War,* p. 37; Ramsaye, *A Million and One Nights,* p. 727. See also "Vitagraph Sues Ford for $1,000,000," *Moving Picture World,* September 8, 1916, p. 1667. Vitagraph, incidentally, dropped the suit after Ford's turn-around when America declared war.

64. Thomas Dixon to Wilson, September 5, 1915, Ser. 4, File 2247, Wilson Papers, Reel 332.

65. "America Invaded Again in Films," *New York Times,* June 7, 1916, p. 11, c. 1. The *Times* reviewer felt that Dixon's convoluted plot could make the audience "laugh all the rest of the picture to scorn." See also Julian Johnson, "The Shadow Stage," *Photoplay,* X, No. 1 (August, 1916), p. 135. Johnson calls *The Fall of a Nation* "'The Battle Cry of Peace' with the punch taken out."

66. Wilson to Dixon, September 7, 1915, Ser. 3, Vol. 24, Wilson Papers, Reel 143.

67. Dixon told Wilson he had arranged for *The Fall of a Nation* to be serialized in the Philadelphia *North American* and the *Chicago Tribune.* Dixon to Wilson, September 5, 1915, Ser. 4, File 2247, Wilson Papers, Reel 332. See also Raymond Cook, *Thomas Dixon,* Sylvia E. Bowman, ed., Twayne's United States Author Series, Vol. 235 (New York: Twayne Publishers, 1965), p. 118.

68. "America Preparing," *New York Times,* July 11, 1916, p. 9, c. 4, and "Uncle Sam's Defenders," *Moving Picture World,* December 9, 1916, p. 1478.

69. Review, "If My Country Should Call," *Moving Picture World,* September 16, 1916, p. 1823.

70. "Liberty, New Preparedness Serial," *Moving Picture World,* July 22, 1916, p. 644. Advertisement, "The Secret of the Submarine," *Moving Picture World,* April 29, 1916, pp. 739–740. Review, "For Uncle Sam's Navy," *Moving Picture World,* June 3, 1916, p. 1755.

71. "Pathe Plans Big Campaign," *Moving Picture World,* December 9, 1916, p. 1479.

72. "Marines in Haiti in Film," *New York Times,* April 26, 1915, p. 11, c. 2; "Unpreparedness Pictured," *New York Times,* February 16, 1916, p. 3, c. 2.

73. Lewis J. Selznick to Wilson, February 14, 1916; and J. C. Drum to Tumulty, February 18, 1916; both in Ser. 4, File 72, Wilson Papers, Reel 198.

74. See Memorandum, Wilson to Tumulty, undated but acknowledged May 20, 1916; Tumulty to Wilson, May 19, 1916; Memorandum, Wilson to Tumulty, undated but April, 1916; and Lawrence E. Rubel to Wilson, May 24, 1916; all in Ser. 4, File 72, Wilson Papers, Reel 199.

75. Rufus Steele to Tumulty, May 27, 1916; Josephus Daniels to Tumulty, May 19, 1916; J. W. Binder, executive director of the Motion Picture Board of Trade, to Tumulty, May 3, 1916; Howard E. Coffin to Tumulty, May 15, 1916; all in Ser. 4, File 72, Wilson Papers, Reel 199.
   For additional information on the film see Julian Johnson, "The Eagle's Wings," *Photoplay,* VI, No. 3 (February, 1917), p. 79; and a plot summary in *Moving Picture World,* December 9, 1916, p. 1552.

76. Jacobs, *Rise of the American Film,* pp. 248–249; see also Jack Spears, "World War I on the Screen," *Films in Review,* Part. 1 (April, 1968), pp. 274–365; Timothy J. Lyons, "Hollywood and W. W. I, 1914–1918," *Journal of Popular Film,* Vol. I, No. 1 (Winter, 1972), pp. 15–30; Creighton Peet, "Hollywood at War, 1915–1918," *Esquire* (September, 1936), p. 60.

**Chapter 3**

1.  George Creel, *Complete Report of the Chairman of the Committee on Public Information, 1917, 1918, 1919* (Washington: Government Printing Office, 1920), p. 47. Cited hereafter as *Complete Report.*

2.  Robert Lansing, Newton Baker, and Josephus Daniels to Woodrow Wilson, April 13, 1917, Ser. 4, File 3856, Wilson Papers, Reel 335. See also James R. Mock and Cedric Larson, *Words That Won the War: The Story of the Committee on Public Information, 1917–1919* (Princeton: Princeton University Press, 1939). Cited hereafter as *Words That Won.* For a comprehensive examination of the origins of the CPI see Stephen Vaughn, *Holding Fast the Inner Lines: Democracy, Nationalism and the Committee on Public Information* (Chapel Hill: University of North Carolina Press, 1980). Cited hereafter as *Holding Fast.*

3.  George Creel, *How We Advertised America: The First Telling of the Amazing Story of the Committee on Public Information That Carried the Gospel of Americanism to Every Corner of the Globe* (New York: Harper and Bros., 1920), p. 4.
    Although Creel always stressed publicity over censorship, many historians believe that Wilson was initially sold on the idea of the CPI because of the need to restrict certain types of military information. See, for example, Mock and Larson, *Words,* pp. 48–51; Hilderbrand, "Power and the People," pp. 354–356.

4.  George Creel, *Rebel at Large: Recollections of Fifty Crowded Years* (New York: G. P. Putnam's Sons, 1947), pp. 156–157. Cited hereafter as *Rebel.*

5.  Quoted in Cedric Larson and James R. Mock, "Lost Files of the Creel Committee of 1917–1919," *Public Opinion Quarterly,* V (January, 1939), p. 10. See also E. David Cronon, ed. *The Cabinet Diaries of Josephus Daniels, 1913–1921* (Lincoln: University of Nebraska Press, 1963), p. 115 and pp. 133–135; and James R. Mock, *Censorship 1917* (Princeton: Princeton University Press, 1941), pp. 42–53.

6.  Creel, *Rebel,* p. 148. For an excellent account of Creel's interest in progressive reforms see Vaughn, *Holding Fast,* pp. 23–38.

7.  George Creel, *Wilson and the Issues* (New York: The Century Company, 1916), p. 37. See also Larson and Mock, "Lost Files," p. 8.

8.  Creel, *Complete Report.* For a much briefer explanation of the CPI's confusing organizational structure, see Mock and Larson, *Words That Won,* pp. 66–74.

9.  Carl Laemmle to Wilson, April 25, 1917, Ser. 4, File 72, Wilson Papers, Reel 199.

10. "Boosting the Liberty Loan," *Moving Picture World,* June 2, 1917, p. 1419. Wooley flattered the movie men with the statement: "There are two great mediums of publicity, the press and the motion pictures."

11. "Industry Backing Liberty Loan," *Moving Picture World,* June 9, 1917, p. 1617. Even before the U. S. entered the war, the film industry sensed that the movies might play a role in the war effort. See "Patriotism and Nature," *Moving Picture World,* March 13, 1917, p. 2702, and "Movies for Preparedness," *New York Times,* March 16, 1917, p. 6, c. 4.

12. William A. Brady to Wilson, June 28, 1917; and Memorandum, Creel to Tumulty, undated but attached to Brady's letter; both in Ser. 4, File 72, Wilson Papers, Reel 199. Creel, incidentally, suggests that the industry war committee has already been formed and that "Brady and the rest are eager for recognition."

13. Wilson to Brady, June 28, 1917, Ser. 4, File 72, Wilson Papers, Reel 199.

14. For an excellent account of Griffith's work in this period see Brownlow, *The War*, pp. 144-155.

15. "Activities of the War Committees of the Motion Picture Industry," *Moving Picture World*, September 22, 1917, p. 1822. See also "Film Interests Mobilized," *New York Times*, July 12, 1917, p. 2, c. 2. and "Movies Mobilized to Aid in War Work," *New York Times*, July 29, 1917, Sec. II, p. 8, c. 2.

16. "Films for Allied Soldiers," *New York Times*, October 7, 1917, Sec. I, p. 7, c. 3.

17. "American Cinema Commission Preparing," *Moving Picture World*, November 10, 1917, p. 842.

18. William Brady to George Creel, August 28, 1917; Patrick Powers to Creel, September 28, 1917; and Creel to Brady, October 1, 1917; all in 1-A1, CPI Records, Record Group 63, National Archives. Cited hereafter as R.G., N.A.

19. Creel, *Complete Report*, pp. 147-148.

20. U.S. Congress, House, Committee on Ways and Means, *Theater Taxes*, Hearings, 66th Cong., 1st Sess., October 7, 1919 (Washington: Government Printing Office, 1919), pp. 38-39. Cited hereafter as *Theater Taxes*. See also, "Government Gives Enthusiastic Approval," *Moving Picture World*, September 23, 1918, p. 1855.

21. Some of this work has been preserved on film. See *Liberty Loan Drives*, Signal Corps Historical Film No. 1133, Record Group 111, National Archives. See also "Liberty Bond Sales," *New York Times*, June 6, 1917, p. 3, c. 4; "Film Folk Doing Their Bit," *Photoplay* (September, 1917), p.111; Cal York, "Plays and Players," *Photoplay* (September, 1917), p. 110; Mock and Larson, *Words That Won*, pp. 132-135; "The Industry and Liberty Bonds," *Moving Picture World*, June 23, 1917, p. 1946.

22. "The Great Liberty Bond Hold-Up," *Photoplay* (December, 1917), p. 58. A clip from this film is in *The Moving Picture Boys in the Great War*, Post-Newsweek Television Stations, Inc./Blackhawk Films.

23. Based on viewing print of *The Bond*, Library of Congress/American Film Institute Collection, Washington, D.C. Cited hereafter as LC/AFI Collection.

24. See letter from Creel to R. M. Hurd of the American Defense Society, reproduced in Creel, *How We Advertised*, p. 447. See also Mock and Larson, *Words That Won*, p. 19 and p. 153, which recounts Wilson's reaction to James Gerard's *My Four Years in Germany*. See also Brownlow, *The War*, p. 130.

25. Based on viewing print of *On Dangerous Ground* in the LC/AFI Collection; see review, "On Dangerous Ground," *Moving Picture World*, January 13, 1917, p. 239.

26. Cyrus Townsend Brady to Wilson, March 4, 1917; Wilson to Tumulty, March 24, 1917; and George F. Lenehan, the branch manager of Vitagraph, to Wilson, March 29, 1917; all in Ser. 4, File 72, Wilson Papers, Reel 199. Lenehan told the president that Newton Baker and Josephus Daniels had endorsed the film, and that Douglas MacArthur, then in the Army Corps of Engineers, had called the film "the most wonderful picture he has ever seen."

27. Review, "Mothers of France," *Moving Picture World*, March 10, 1917, p. 1447.

28. For a fine plot summary see Brownlow, *The War*, pp. 131-134; see also Edward Weitzel, "The Little American," *Moving Picture World*, July 21, 1917, p. 471. Later in the war

Pickford starred in another propaganda film, *Johanna Enlists*. A partial print of the film is in the LC/AFI Collection in Washington, and a print of Pickford's *The Little American* is in the George Eastman House, Rochester, New York.

29. Based on print of *The Man Who Was Afraid* in the LC/AFI Collection. The film was directed by Fred Wright.

30. Based on print of *The Kingdom of Hope* in the LC/AFI Collection.

31. Brownlow, *The War*, p. 135.

32. Based on print of *Swat the Spy* at Blackhawk Films, Davenport, Iowa. See also review, "Swat the Spy," *Moving Picture World*, September 21, 1918, p. 1156.

33. Based on print of *Spying the Spy* in the LC/AFI Collection (1 reel).

34. Based on print of *Shoulder Arms* in the LC/AFI Collection.

35. Based on a partial print of *Doing His Bit* in the LC/AFI Collection.

36. Based on print of *Yankee Doodle in Berlin* at Blackhawk Films, Davenport, Iowa.

37. Based on print of *My Four Years in Germany* at the Em Gee Film Library, Santa Monica, California.

38. Mock and Larson, *Words That Won*, p. 153.

39. Brownlow, *The War*, p. 137.

40. Lyons, "Hollywood and World War I," p. 22.

41. Based on print of *The Unbeliever* in the LC/AFI Collection.

42. Based on print of *Heart of Humanity* at Blackhawk Films, Davenport, Iowa.

43. Telegram, D. W. Griffith to Tumulty, March 29, 1918, Ser. 4, File 72, Wilson Papers, Reel 199.

44. Arthur Friend to Tumulty, June 1, 1918, Ser. 4, File 80, Wilson Papers, Reel 200.

45. Telegram, D. W. Griffith to Mrs. Woodrow Wilson, June 14, 1918, Ser. 4, File 541, Wilson Papers, Reel 285.

46. Ibid.

47. Brownlow, *The War*, pp. 153–154; see also note, Wilson to Tumulty, June 14, 1918; Albert Grey to Mrs. Wilson, June 19, 1918; and attached note, undated, but June, Wilson to Tumulty; all in Ser. 4, File 541, Wilson Papers, Reel 285.

48. "Essanay Cuts Out Depressing Stories," *Moving Picture World*, June 9, 1917, p. 1605; and William H. Jackson, "War Time Pictures," *Moving Picture World*, August 24, 1917, p. 769.

49. Newton D. Baker, "Letter From the Secretary of War Transmitting Information Regarding the Taking and Exhibition of Still and Moving Pictures of War Preparations and of the American Expeditionary Force," House Doc. No. 1227, July 10, 1918, 65th Cong., 2nd Sess., referred to the Committee on Military Affairs, July 12, 1918, p. 2.

50. *Annual Report of the Chief Signal Officer, United States Army, to the Secretary of War* (Washington: Government Printing Office, 1919), pp. 341–342. Cited hereafter as *Annual Report CSO*. See also Mould's excellent account in *American Newsfilm*, Chapter 9, and Brownlow's *The War*, pp. 119–130.

51. "War Pictures for America," *New York Times*, October 28, 1917, Sec. I, p. 17, c. 1. See also "Annual Report CSO," p. 345.

52. *Annual Report CSO*, p. 362; and K. Jack Bauer, comp. *List of World War I Signal Corps Films*, SL 14, General Services Administration, National Archives and Records Service (Washington, 1957), p. 1. Cited hereafter as *Signal Corps List*.

53. *Annual Report CSO*, p. 362; see also "Monthly Report to the Chief Signal Officer for December of 1917," January 1, 1918, File 321.4, Records of the American Expeditionary Forces (World War I), 1917–1919, Record Group 120, National Archives. Cited hereafter as Records of AEF, R.G. 120, N.A.

54. Bauer, *Signal Corps List*, p. 1; see also Brownlow, *The War*, p. 125. Brownlow's account is based, in part, on interviews with Signal Corps cameramen Ernest B. Schoedsack, Irvin Willat, and George Marshall.

55. Creel, *How We Advertised*, p. 119.

56. "Report of the Photographic Subsection," May 1, 1919, in *United States Army in the World War, 1917–1919: Reports of the Commander-in-Chief, AEF*, Staff Sections and Services, Historical Division, Department of the Army (Washington: Government Printing Office, 1948), p. 131. Cited hereafter as *Subsection Report*.

57. Bauer, *Signal Corps List*, p. 1; and "Monthly Report to the Chief Signal Officer for March of 1918," April 1, 1918, File 321.94, Records of AEF, R.G. 120, N.A.

58. *Annual Report CSO*, p. 342.

59. Brownlow, *The War*, pp. 119–130. Among others Brownlow mentions Lewis Milestone, Alan Crosland, Joseph Sternberg and George Marshall.

60. Bauer, *Signal Corps List*, p. 1; and *Annual Report CSO*, p. 343.

61. "Monthly Reports to the Chief Signal Officer for January and February of 1918," File 321.94, Records of AEF, R.G. 120, N.A.

62. "Photographic Bulletin No. 2," Headquarters of the AEF, Office of the Chief Signal Officer, Photographic Division, August 1, 1918, File 004.5, Records of AEF, R.G. 120, N.A.

63. *Annual Report CSO*, p. 114 and p. 342.

64. Ibid., p. 114.

65. Captain Paul Miller, "Report of the Photo Lab," November 20, 1917, File 233.00, Records of AEF, R.G. 120, N.A. See also "Monthly Report to the Chief Signal Officer for September of 1917," October 1, 1917, File 321.94, Records of AEF, R.G. 120, N.A.

66. A copy of this syllabus was attached to "Monthly Report to the Chief Signal Officer for March of 1918," April 1, 1918, File 321.94, Records of AEF, R.G. 120, N.A.

67. "Photographic Bulletin No. 4," Headquarters of AEF, Office of the Chief Signal Officer, Photographic Division, August 6, 1918, File 004.5, Records of AEF, R.G. 120, N.A.

68. *Annual Report CSO*, p. 344.

69. Ibid., p. 346. For some firsthand accounts of the problems faced in shooting this type of film see "War Cameraman's Kit," *Moving Picture World*, December 15, 1917, p. 1673; Geoffrey Malins, *How I Filmed the War* (New York: Stokes, [1919]).

70. Creel, *How We Advertised*, p. 119.

71. Creel, *Complete Report*, p. 61.

72. Creel, *How We Advertised*, p. 118; see also Office Order No. 3, November 12, 1917, Office of the Chief Signal Officer, War Department, File 004.5, Records of the AEF, R.G. 120, N.A.; see also Creel to Banning, June 21, 1918, 1–A1, CPI Records, R.G. 63, N.A.

73. Creel, *How We Advertised*, p. 118.

74. Mock and Larson, *Words That Won*, p. 136; Vaughn, *Holding Fast*, p. 204, who mentions Mack but places Hart in the Division of Films at the same time.

75. Ibid. See also Creel, *How We Advertised*, p. 119. Creel makes no mention of Mack in his *Complete Report*.

76. Louis Mack to Creel, April 8, 1918, 1–A1, CPI Records, R.G. 63, N.A. Mack told Creel: "We have at all times endeavored to operate so as not to have the government conflict with the business of commercial producers; we desired the good will of the latter and have at all times received it."

77. Creel, *Complete Report*, p. 48; see also "Balfour Arouses Big War Benefit," *New York Times*, May 13, 1917, p. 3, c. 1.; "Show Tanks in Action," *New York Times*, May 21, 1917, p. 7, c. 6.

78. Creel, *Complete Report*, pp. 47–48.

79. "Patriotic and Red Cross Films," *Moving Picture World*, June 16, 1917, p. 1605, provided a list with some of the following titles: *The American Soldier in the Philippines* (Educational Film Corp.), *Uncle Sam Awake* (Regson Film Corp.), *Making Our Navy* (Mutual-Rothacker), *Making a United States Soldier* (Universal-Powers), and *How Uncle Sam Prepares* (Pioneer Film Corp.).

80. Meryl LaVoy to Wilson, July 19, 1917, Ser. 4, File 72, Wilson Papers, Reel 199; see also "Balfour Arouses Big War Benefit," *New York Times*, May 13, 1917, p. 3, c. 1; and see Evan Evans of the Red Cross Bureau of Motion Pictures to Creel, 1–A5, CPI Records, R.G. 63, N.A.

81. Capt. Joe T. Marshall to Paul D. Rainey, September 15, 1917, File 004.5, Records of AEF, R.G. 120, N.A.

82. Paul Rainey to Major Nolan, June 22, 1917, File 004.5, Records of AEF, R.G. 120, N.A.

83. Major F. Palmer to Paul Rainey, September 15, 1917, File 004.5, Records of AEF, R.G. 63, N.A.

84. George Creel to Evan Evans of the Red Cross Motion Picture Bureau, October 26, 1917, 1–A5, CPI Records, R.G. 63, N.A.

85. "Scope and Activities of the Committee on Public Information Shown in Report by Chairman Creel Made to President," January 7, 1918, 1–B2, CPI Records, R.G. 63, N.A. See also U.S. Congress, House, Subcommittee on Appropriations, *Sundry Civil Bill, 1919*, Hearings, 65th Cong., 2nd Sess., Pt. III (Washington: Government Printing Office, 1918), pp. 70–71. Cited hereafter as *Sundry Civil Bill 1919*.

86. "Scope and Activities," January 7, 1918, 1–B2, CPI Records, R.G. 63, N.A.

## Chapter 4

1. Creel to William A. Johnston, January 28, 1918, 1–A1, CPI Records, R.G. 63, N.A.

2. William Johnston to Creel, January 18, 1918, 1–A1, CPI Records, R.G. 63, N.A.

3. Brownlow, *The War*, p. 116.

4. Johnston to Creel, January 18, 1918, 1–A1, CPI Records, R.G. 63, N.A. See also Creel, *How We Advertised*, p. 247.

5. Creel, *Rebel*, pp. 133–139.

6. Creel to Johnston, January 28, 1918, 1–A1, CPI Records, R.G. 63, N.A. See also memorandum Creel to L. E. Rubel, undated but attached to Johnston letter above.

7. Laurence E. Rubel to Joseph Marshall, Chief of Photographic Section, January 25, 1918, File 004.5, Records of AEF, R.G. 120, N.A.

8. Telegram, Carl Byoir to Louis Mack, April 8, 1918, 1–A5, CPI Records, R.G. 63, N.A. See also Mack to Creel, April 8, 1918 and Creel to Mack, April 10, 1918; both in 1–A1, CPI Records, R.G. 63, N.A.

9. William Randolph Hearst to Creel, March 13, 1918, 1–A1, CPI Records, R.G. 63, N.A. "You took Sisson, the editor of *Cosmopolitan,*" Hearst told Creel, "and I did not complain, although we missed him greatly; but Hart is a loss I do not know how to replace."

10. Mock and Larson, *Words That Won*, p. 136.

11. Creel, *Complete Report*, p. 13.

12. Ibid.

13. *Pershing's Crusaders*, Signal Corps Historical Film No. 1213, Records of the Office of the Chief Signal Officer, Record Group 111, National Archives. Cited hereafter as R.G. 111, N.A.

14. *America's Answer*, Signal Corps Historical Film No. 316, R.G. 111, N.A.

15. Charles Hart to Bruce Barton, March 28, 1918, 10A–A1, CPI Records, R.G. 63, N.A.

16. Continuity sheets for *Pershing's Crusaders*, R.G. 111, N.A.

17. Ramsaye, *A Million and One Nights*, pp. 784–795. Several existing copies of the *Official War Review* are in the Ford Collection in the National Archives. See, for example, Issue 18 (FC 200.54) and Issue 19 (FC 200.48).

18. Ibid., p. 782; and see Ralph Wolfe of the Red Cross Bureau of Pictures to L. E. Rubel, March 30, 1918; Memorandum, Rubel to Carl Byoir, April 1, 1918; both in 30–A1, CPI Records, R.G. 63, N.A.

19. Memorandum, Jane S. Johnson to Charles Hart, April 10, 1918, 10A–A1, CPI Records, R.G. 63, N.A.

20. Creel to president of Kineto Company of America, April 18, 1918, 10A–A1, CPI Records, R.G. 63, N.A.

21. Charles Hart to Edmund Ratisbonne, April 12, 1918, 20–A1, CPI Records, R.G. 63, N.A.

22. Hart to Creel, March 28, 1918, 30–A1, CPI Records, R.G. 63, N.A.

23. *Sundry Civil Bill 1919*, p. 76; see also Henry C. Carr, "Capturing the Kaiser," *Photoplay* (March, 1916), pp. 111–112; and review, "On the Firing Line with the Germans," *Moving Picture World*, January 5, 1916, p. 481.

24. William Brady to Creel, May 2, 1918, and Creel to Adolph Zukor, November 23, 1917; both in 1–A1, CPI Records, R.G. 63, N.A.

25. Hart to Creel, March 28, 1918, 30–A1, CPI Records, R.G. 63, N.A.

26. "Film Division Names Director Advisors," *Moving Picture World*, July 20, 1918, p. 363. This advisory board from the Motion Picture Director's Association was composed of J. Searle Dawley (chair), Maurice Tourneur, Raoul A. Walsh, Charles Giblyn, Edwin Carewe, James Vincent and Sidney Olcott. See also Hart to J. Searle Dawley, May 13, 1918, 10A–1A, CPI Records. R.G. 63, N.A.

27. E. B. Hatrick to Major A. L. James, officer in charge, Photographic Subsection G-1-D, May 23, 1918, File 004.5211, Records of AEF, R.G. 120, N.A.

28. *Subsection Report*, p. 132.

29. Captain William E. Moore to Lieut. Colonel W. C. Sweeny, September 9, 1918, File 004.5211, Records of AEF, R.G. 120, N.A.

30. Lieut. Joseph T. Marshall to Lieut. Colonel W. C. Sweeny, May 1, 1918, File 004.5211, Records of AEF, R.G. 120, N.A.

31. Captain Robert Warwick to Lieut. Colonel W. C. Sweeny, June 3, 1918, File 004.5211, Records of AEF, R.G. 120, N.A.

32. Captain Robert Warwick to Lieut. Colonel W. C. Sweeny, July 26, 1918, File 004.5211, Records of AEF, R.G. 120, N.A.

33. Warwick to Sweeny, June 3, 1918. See also "America's Answer Stirs War Spirit," *New York Times*, July 30, 1918, p. 9, c. 3. The new titles for *America's Answer* were written by Kenneth C. Beaton.

34. Rufus Steele, "Progress Report of the Department of Scenarios," August 10, 1918, 1–B1, CPI Records, R.G. 63, N.A.

35. Ibid., p. 3.

36. Ibid., pp. 2–3.

37. Creel, *Complete Report*, p. 57. Chester's one-reel pictures were: *Schooling Our Fighting Mechanics, There Shall Be No Cripples, Colored Americans, It's an Engineer's War, Finding and Fixing the Enemy, Waging War in Washington, All the Comforts of Home, Master for the Merchant Marine, The College for Camp Cooks,* and *Railless Railroads.* See also "Standardizing Travel Pictures," *Moving Picture World*, September 2, 1916, p. 1516.

38. Creel, *Complete Report*, pp. 57–58.

39. Ibid. For the same reason, the Scenario Department was forced to cancel six more two-reel pictures that it had begun planning prior to the armistice.

40. Creel, *How We Advertised*, p. 120.

41. Ramsaye, *A Million and One Nights*, p. 783.

42. Telegram, Charles Hart to Creel, April 11, 1918, 30–A1, CPI Records, R.G. 63, N.A.

43. Hart to James Sheldon of the Mutual Film Corporation, May 7, 1918, 10A-A1, CPI Records, R.G. 63, N.A. The CPI rejected an offer from the newsreel companies to pay $2,650 for a weekly supply of 2,000 feet of official war films.

44. Creel, *How We Advertised*, pp. 123–124.

45. Creel, *Complete Report*, p. 54.

46. Ibid.

47. Creel, *How We Advertised*, pp. 122–123.

48. Review, "America's Answer," *New York Times*, July 30, 1918, p. 9, c. 3.

49. Creel, *The Complete Report*, p. 51. Pathe distributed the *Official War Review*. The First National Exhibitor's Circuit handled *Pershing's Crusaders* and the Downing Film Company, *Our Colored Fighters*. William Brady's World Film Corporation distributed three CPI films: *America's Answer, Under Four Flags*, and the *U.S.A. Series*.

50. Ibid., p. 52.

51. "Pershing's Bookings Largest Ever," *Moving Picture World*, September 21, 1918, p. 1703; "Go over the Top with Pershing," *Moving Picture World*, July 27, 1918, p. 358; "Race for the World's Trophy on," *Moving Picture World*, July 27, 1918, p. 531. The number of bookings obtained for *Pershing's Crusaders* was soon eclipsed by the bookings for *America's Answer*.

52. Creel, *Complete Report*, p. 53.

53. Ibid., p. 54.

54. Ibid., pp. 52–54. These figures do not include bookings for CPI films in the three states— North Dakota, Michigan, and California—where the state councils of defense distributed the CPI films.

55. Ibid., p. 49. See also Mock and Larson, *Words That Won*, p. 141.

56. U.S. Congress, House, Committee on Ways and Means, *Theater Taxes*, Hearings, 66th Cong., 1st Sess., October 7, 1919 (Washington: Government Printing Office, 1919), pp. 37–39. Cited hereafter as *Theater Taxes 1919*.

**Chapter 5**

1. Creel, *How We Advertised*, p. 4.

2. Some of the best sources on censorship in World War I are: James R. Mock, *Censorship 1917* (Princeton: Princeton University Press, 1941); and Zechariah Chafee, *Freedom of Speech* (New York: Harcourt, Brace, and Co., 1920).
   The Espionage Act is found in C. 30, 40 *Stat.* 217; the Sedition Act in C. 75, Sec. 1, 40 *Stat.* 533. For the Trading-with-the-Enemy Act see C. 106, 40 *Stat.* 411.

3. Mock and Larson, *Words That Won*, pp. 20–21.

4. Mock, *Censorship 1917*, pp. 57–60.

5. U.S. Committee on Public Information, "Information Concerning the Making and Distributing of Pictures that Show the Activities of the Army and Navy" (Washington:

Government Printing Office), pp. 3–7. A copy of this pamphlet is located in 1–B1, CPI Records, R.G. 63, N.A.

6.  Mock and Larson, *Words That Won,* pp. 148–150.

7.  "Patria," *Moving Picture World,* December 9, 1916, p. 1237. Other accounts of the *Patria* case can be found in Mock and Larson, pp. 143–147 and Mock, *Censorship 1917,* p. 175.

8.  William Redfield to Wilson, June 1, 1917, Ser. 4, File 4020, Wilson Papers, Reel 360.

9.  Wilson to J. A. Berst, June 15, 1917, Ser. 4, File 4020, Wilson Papers, Reel 360.

10. J. A. Berst to Wilson, June 18, 1917, Ser. 4, File 4020, Wilson Papers, Reel 359.

11. Wilson to Berst, August 11, 1917, Ser. 4, File 4020, Wilson Papers, Reel 359.

12. See Berst to Wilson, August 16, 1917; Wilson to Berst, August 21, 1917; Genville S. MacFarland to Wilson, August 23, 1917; Robert Lansing to Tumulty, September 1, 1917; Memorandum Wilson to Tumulty, undated but September, 1917; Lansing to Tumulty, October 4, 1917; all in Ser. 4, File 4020, Wilson Papers, Reel 359.

13. Mock, *Censorship 1917,* pp. 183–184.

14. Ibid., p. 185.

15. This letter is reproduced in Mock and Larson, *Words That Won,* pp. 148–149.

16. Mock, *Censorship 1917,* p. 173. Vitagraph's response was to recall all prints of the film and to release a new version of the film entitled *The Battle Cry of War.*

17. See, for example, J. M. Shellman, "Maryland Censors Recall War Films," *Moving Picture World,* May 12, 1917, p. 992; Kenneth C. Crain, "Ohio Censors Watch All War Films Closely," *Moving Picture World,* May 19, 1917, p. 1464; and J. L. Ray, "Mayor's Order Stops All War Pictures," *Moving Picture World,* June 23, 1917, p. 1974.

18. Mock, *Censorship 1917,* p. 176; see also "Bans All Films That Discourage Enlistment," *Moving Picture World,* May 5, 1917, p. 832.

19. Brownlow, *The War,* pp. 80–82. See also Mock, *Censorship 1917,* pp. 179–181.

20. Ibid.

21. *Goldstein vs. United States,* 258 Fed. 908 (9th Cir., 1919). See also *United States vs. The Motion Picture Film "The Spirit of '76,"* 252 Fed. 9467 (S.D. California, 1917).

22. Creel, *How We Advertised,* pp. 273–282; Mock and Larson, *Words That Won,* pp. 235–334; Creel to Paul Fuller, Jr., January 4, 1918, 1–A1, CPI Records, R.G. 63, N.A.

23. Creel to Paul Fuller, Jr., January 14, 1918, 1–A1, CPI Records, R.G. 63, N.A.

24. Creel, *How We Advertised,* p. 276.

25. Creel, *Complete Report,* p. 7.

26. Creel, *How We Advertised,* p. 277.

27. Ibid., p. 281. See also "Export Regulations" in *The War Trade Board Journal,* July 10, 1918, p. 11, located in the CPI files, 1–B1, CPI Records, R.G. 63, N.A.

28. See "Card Record of Films Received and Passed for Export, May–December, 1918," 30–B1 and B2; and "Card Record of Films Rejected for Export to Foreign Countries, May–October, 1918," 30–B3, both in CPI Records, R.G. 63, N.A.

29.  Ibid.

30.  "Memorandum on Motion Picture Accounts," July 10, 1916, Price, Waterhouse and Company, New York, p. 12.

31.  See "Working Agreement between the Committee on Public Information and the Export Division of the National Association of the Motion Picture Industry," attached to William Brady to Creel, July 12, 1918, 1–A1, CPI Records, R.G. 63, N.A.

32.  U.S. Congress, House, Subcommittee on Appropriations, *Sundry Civil Bill, 1919,* Hearings, 65th Cong., 2nd Sess., Pt. III (Washington: Government Printing Office, 1918), p. 78. See also, Creel, *How We Advertised,* pp. 14–15 and p. 68.

33.  "Funds for Creel Reduced by House," *New York Times,* June 18, 1918, p. 7, c. 1. Creel had asked for $2,098,000 and received $1,250,000. See also "Creel Accepts Congress Control," *New York Times,* June 14, 1918, p. 8, c. 3.

    See also Walton E. Bean, "George Creel and His Critics: A Study of the Attacks on the Committee on Public Information, 1917–1919" (unpublished Ph.D. dissertation, University of Southern California, 1941). Bean concludes that most of the attacks on Creel and the CPI were partisan, citing the fact that of the 32 Congressmen who made public attacks on Creel, all but four were Republicans.

34.  "Creel Cuts Back Work," *New York Times,* July 10, 1918, p. 9, c. 2; "Creel to Lose Draft Age Men," *New York Times,* June 27, 1918, p. 5, c. 1.

35.  "Army to Investigate Hearst's Tank Film," *New York Times,* June 25, 1918, p. 24, c. 2. The Hearst papers, incidentally, had been banned in Canada and Britain because of their alleged pro-German sentiments.

36.  Raymond B. Fosdick to Wilson, October 15, 1917, Ser. 4, File 72, Wilson Papers, Reel 199. The gap between Powers and Fosdick can best be illustrated by Fosdick's statement that the soldiers did not want to see "sob stuff about mother, home, and heaven, nor glorious war films showing the soldiers as especially heroic." It sounds as if Mr. Fosdick had been seeing a few of the industry's more propagandistic "war films."

    See also W. H. Jackson, "War Time Picture Activities," *Moving Picture World,* August 11, 1917, p. 924. Fosdick's plan involved the Y.M.C.A. and the Community Motion Picture Bureau headed by Warren Dunham Foster. With the help of the Klaw and Erlanger projector company, Foster had outfitted trucks with portable projectors that could be driven right into the military camps. See also, "Motor Car Movies," *New York Times,* August 20, 1917, p. 5, c. 1.

37.  "War Film Stopped; Hearst Influence on Creel Blamed," *New York Times,* June 29, 1918, p. 1, c. 1.

38.  "Aeroplane Clash between Creel and Universal," *Moving Picture World,* July 6, 1918, pp. 41–42. See also "Truce in Universal-Creel Row," *Moving Picture World,* July 6, 1918, p. 62.

39.  "War Film Stopped," p. 1, c. 2. This list included four men—Charles Hart, Carl Byoir, Edgar Sisson and Ray Hall—who had worked with various Hearst newspapers and magazines. The remainder of the men had been associated with the Hearst-Pathe newsreel or with Hearst's International Film Service: J. A. Berst, H. C. Hoagland, E. B. Hatrick, Lew Simons, C. F. Van Arsdale, G. A. Smith, Hubell and Donahue.

40.  "Call Truce in Fight over Suppressed Film," *New York Times,* June 25, 1918, p. 24, c. 3. See also "Brunet Denies Statements of Universal," *Moving Picture World,* July 6, 1918, p. 42.

41. "Army to Investigate Hearst's Tank Film," *New York Times,* June 25, 1918, p. 24, c. 2.

42. "Call Truce in Fight," *New York Times,* p. 35.

43. Mock and Larson, *Words That Won,* p. 150.

44. House Res. 402, *Congressional Record,* 65th Cong., 2nd Sess., June 25, 1918, p. 8284; June 29, 1918, p. 8536. See also "Wants Baker to Tell of Film Agreement," *New York Times,* June 26, 1918, p. 7, c. 1; "Congressmen Inquire About Picturemaking," *Moving Picture World,* July 13, 1918, p. 201; "Attacks Creel Committee," *New York Times,* April 2, 1918, p. 7, c. 7. Treadway said that the CPI should be called the "Committee on Misinformation."

45. "Creel Declines to Appear," *New York Times,* June 28, 1918, p. 8, c. 7.

46. "Creel Explains Films," *New York Times,* June 29, 1918, p. 6, c. 2; "Explanations Clear War-Films Row," *Moving Picture World,* July 13, 1918, p. 201.

47. Newton D. Baker, "Letter from the Secretary of War Transmitting Information Regarding the Taking and Exhibition of Still and Moving Pictures of War Preparations of the American Expeditionary Forces," House Doc. No. 1227, July 10, 1918, 65th Cong., 2nd Sess., referred to the Committee on Military Affairs, July 12, 1918, pp. 1–6.

48. "Managers Fight Three-Day Closing," *Moving Picture World,* January 26, 1918, p. 537; "Black Tuesdays Mean Good Mondays," *Moving Picture World,* February 9, 1918; "Theaters Dazed, Rally Quickly," *Moving Picture World,* February 2, 1918, p. 680; Douglas Hawley, "Asking Whether Lightless Nights Save Coal," *Moving Picture World,* January 19, 1918, p. 406; and "Exhibitors Protest Lightless Nights," *Moving Picture World,* January 5, 1918, p. 120.

49. "Plan to Control Industry for War," *New York Times,* April 8, 1918, p. 4, c. 1–3.

50. Telegram, Brady to Creel, May 20, 1918, 1–A1, CPI Records, R.G. 63, N.A.

51. Creel to William G. McAdoo, Herbert Hoover, and H. A. Garfield, May 23, 1918, 1–A1, CPI Records, R.G. 63, N.A.

52. See "Brief—Presenting Reasons, Facts and Arguments for Declaring the Motion Picture Industry as an Essential Industry by the Government," attached to William A. Brady to Tumulty, August 30, 1918, Ser. 4, File 72, Wilson Papers, N.A. The NAMPI's brief is 26 pages long. See also McAdoo and Hoover to Creel, May 25, 1918; both in 1–A1, CPI Records, R.G. 63, N.A.

53. Telegram, William Brady to Tumulty, June 5, 1918, Ser. 4, File 72, Wilson Papers, Reel 199.

54. "Moving Pictures Declared an Essential Industry," *New York Times,* August 26, 1918, p. 9, c. 2; see also "Industry Declared Essential," *Moving Picture World,* September 7, 1918, p. 1386. Under the terms of this agreement the film industry agreed to stop all unnecessary production, to reclaim all old films, to produce only one negative unless a film was to be exported, to stop the construction of all new theaters and to repair projectors and cameras rather than replace them as long as the war continued.

55. "Paul Brunet Discusses Essentiality," *Moving Picture World,* September 28, 1918, p. 1855; "Whole Industry Declared Essential," *Moving Picture News,* September 7, 1918, p. 154.

56. "Most Important Events of the Year," *Wid's Year Book* [Later called *Film Daily Yearbook*] (1918), reprint (New York: Arno Press, 1971), n.p.

57. Quoted in ibid.

**Epilogue**

1. Creel, *How We Advertised,* p. 68.

2. U.S. Congress, House, Committee on Interstate and Foreign Commerce, *Moving Pictures as a Means of Commercial Promotion,* Hearings on House Res. 571, 65th Cong., 3rd Sess., March 1, 1918 (Washington: Government Printing Office, 1919), pp. 1–17.

3. Wilson to Douglas Fairbanks, January 13, 1919, Ser. 5B, Wilson Papers, Reel 289. For offers to provide films for the president's new projector see, Lambert St. Clair to Rudolph Forster, April 1, 1918, Ser. 4, File 4000, Wilson Papers, Reel 359; and Adolph Zukor to Wilson, November 13, 1918, Ser. 4, File 72, Wilson Papers, Reel 199.

4. Tino Ballio, *United Artists: The Company Built by Stars* (Madison: University of Wisconsin Press, 1976), pp. 24–25 and p. 29.

5. For the correspondence which resulted in Wilson's endorsement see William Fox to Wilson, August 21, 1919; Tumulty to Wilson, August 27, 1919 and attached copy of Wilson's letter dated September 2, 1919; all in Ser. 4, File 72, Wilson Papers, Reel 199. A print of this newsreel still exists in the Fox Movietone film archives.

# Bibliography

**Primary Sources**

*Manuscript and film collections*

American Film Institute-Library of Congress, Film Collection. Library of Congress, Washington, D. C.
Blackhawk Films, Film Collection. Davenport, Iowa.
Records of the American Expeditionary Forces (World War I), 1917–1923, Record Group 120, National Archives, Washington, D. C.
Records of the Committee on Public Information, Record Group 63, National Archives, Washington, D. C.
Records of the Office of the Chief Signal Officer, Record Group 111, National Archives, Washington, D. C.
Wilson, Woodrow. Papers. Library of Congress Microfilm.

*Published government documents*

Baker, Newton D. *Letter from the Secretary of War Transmitting Information Regarding the Taking and Exhibition of Still and Moving Pictures of War Preparations and of the American Expeditionary Force.* 65th Cong., 2nd Sess., July 12, 1918, House Doc. 1227. Washington, Government Printing Office, 1918.
Bauer, K. Jack, comp. *List of World War I Signal Corps Films.* SL 14, General Services Administration. National Archives and Records Service. Washington, 1957.
U. S. Army. *Annual Report of the Chief Signal Officer to the Secretary of War.* Washington, Government Printing Office, 1919.
U. S. Army Historical Division. *The United States Army in the World War, 1917–1919: Reports of the Commander-in-Chief, A. E. F., Staff Sections and Services.* Washington, Government Printing Office, 1948.
U. S. Congress. *Congressional Record.*
U. S. Congress. House. Committee on Education. *Bills to Establish a Federal Motion Picture Commission.* Hearings, 63rd Cong., 2nd Sess. Washington, Government Printing Office, 1914.
U. S. Congress. House. Committee on Interstate and Foreign Commerce. *Moving Pictures as a Means of Commercial Promotion.* Hearings pursuant to H. Res. 571, 65th Cong., 3rd Sess., March 1, 1919. Washington, Government Printing Office, 1919.
U. S. Congress. House. Committee on Ways and Means. *Theater Taxes.* Hearings, 65th Cong., 2nd Sess., Pt. III. Washington, Government Printing Office, 1918.

U. S. Congress. House. Committee on Ways and Means, Subcommittee on Appropriations. *Sundry Civil Appropriations Bill for 1919.* Hearings, 65th Cong., 2nd Sess., Pt. III. Washington, Government Printing Office, 1919.

U. S. Congress. Senate. Committee on the Judiciary. *Investigation of Brewing and Liquor Interests and German Propaganda.* Hearings pursuant to S. Res. 307, 65th Cong., 2nd and 3rd Sess., Vol. 2. Washington, Government Printing Office, 1919.

*Memoirs, published letters, biographies and autobiographies*

Baker, Ray S. *Woodrow Wilson: Life and Letters.* 8 vols. Garden City: Doubleday, Doran and Co., 1927–1939.

Creel, George. *Rebel at Large: Recollections of Fifty Crowded Years.* New York: G. P. Putnam's Sons, 1947.

Cronon, E. David, ed. *The Cabinet Diaries of Josephus Daniels, 1913–1921.* Lincoln: University of Nebraska Press, 1963.

Link, Arthur S. *Wilson.* 5 vols. Princeton: Princeton University Press, 1947–1965.

**Secondary Literature**

*General works*

Abel, John. *My Life in the Trenches.* Iowa City: University of Iowa Press, 1978.

Ballio, Tino. *United Artists: The Company Built by Stars.* Madison: The University of Wisconsin Press, 1976.

Brownlow, Kevin. *The War, The West, The Wilderness.* New York: Alfred Knopf, 1978.

Chafee, Zechariah. *Freedom of Speech.* New York: Harcourt, Brace and Company, 1920.

Cook, Raymond. *Thomas Dixon.* ed. Sylvia E. Bowman. Twayne's United States Authors Series, Vol. 235. New York: Twayne Publishers, 1965.

Creel, George. *Complete Report of the Chairman of the Committee on Public Information, 1917, 1918, 1919.* Washington: Government Printing Office, 1920.

———. *How We Advertised America: The First Telling of the Amazing Story of the Committee on Public Information That Carried the Gospel of Americanism to Every Corner of the Globe.* New York: Harper and Bros., 1920.

———. *Wilson and the Issues.* New York: The Century Co., 1916.

Fielding, Raymond. *The American Newsreel, 1911–1967.* Norman: The University of Oklahoma Press, 1972.

Finnegan, John Patrick. *Against the Specter of a Dragon: The Campaign for American Military Preparedness, 1914–1917.* Westport: Greenwood Press, 1974.

Furhammer, Lief, and Folke Isaksson. *Politics and Film.* New York: Praegar Publishers, 1971.

Hampton, Benjamin B. *A History of the American Film Industry: From Its Beginnings to 1931.* 1931; rev. ed. New York: Dover Publications, 1970.

Higham, John. *Strangers in the Land: Patterns of American Nativism.* New York: Atheneum, 1963.

Huettig, Mae D. *Economic Control of the Motion Picture Industry: A Study in Industrial Organization.* Philadelphia: University of Pennsylvania Press, 1944.

Irwin, Will. *The House That Shadows Built.* Garden City: Doubleday, Doran and Co., 1928.

Jacobs, Lewis. *The Rise of the American Film.* New York: Teacher's College Press, 1938.

Jowett, Garth. *Film: The Democratic Art, A Social History of American Film.* Boston: Little, Brown and Co., 1976.

Lewis, Howard T. *The Motion Picture Industry.* New York: D. Van Nostrand Company, 1933.

Link, Arthur S. *Woodrow Wilson and the Progressive Era, 1910-1917.* New York: Harper Torchbooks, 1963.

Malins, Geoffrey. *How I Filmed the War.* New York: Stokes, [1919].

MacCann, Richard D. *The People's Film: A Political History of U.S. Government Motion Pictures.* New York: Hastings House, 1973.

Manvell, Roger, and Heinrich Fraenkel. *The German Cinema.* London: J. M. Dent, 1971.

Maxim, Hudson. *Defenseless America.* New York: Hearst International Library, 1916.

Millis, Walter. *Road to War: America 1914-1917.* Boston: Houghton Mifflin Company, 1935.

Mock, James R. *Censorship 1917.* Princeton: Princeton University Press, 1941.

_____, and Cedric Larson. *Words That Won the War: The Story of the Committee on Public Information, 1917-1919.* Princeton: Princeton University Press, 1939.

Mould, David H. *American Newsfilm, 1914-1919: The Underexposed War.* New York: Garland Publishing, 1983.

Ramsaye, Terry. *A Million and One Nights.* New York: Simon and Schuster, 1926.

Seabury, William H. *The Public and the Motion Picture Industry.* New York: The Macmillan Company, 1926.

Sklar, Robert. *Movie-Made America: A Cultural History of American Movies.* New York: Random House, 1975.

Slide, Anthony. *The Big V: A History of the Vitagraph Company.* Metuchen, N. J.: The Scarecrow Press, 1976.

Vaughn, Stephen. *Holding Fast the Inner Lines: Democracy, Nationalism, and the Committee on Public Information.* Chapel Hill: University of North Carolina Press, 1980.

*Unpublished theses and dissertations*

Bean, Walton E. "George Creel and His Critics: A Study of the Attacks on the Committee on Public Information, 1917-1919," unpublished Ph.D. dissertation, University of Southern California, 1941.

Hilderbrand, Robert C. "Power and the People: Executive Management of Public Opinion in Foreign Affairs, 1869-1921," unpublished Ph.D. dissertation, University of Iowa, 1977.

Ward, Larry W. "The Motion Picture Goes to War: A Political History of the United States Government's Film Effort in the World War, 1914-1918," unpublished Ph.D. dissertation, University of Iowa, 1981.

*Signed articles*

Brunet, Paul. "Paul Brunet Discusses Essentiality," *Moving Picture World,* September 28, 1918, p. 1855.

Bush, W. Stephen. "The Exhibitor's Power," *Moving Picture World,* June 19, 1915, p. 1913.

_____. "Here is Cine-Mundial," *Moving Picture World,* December 17, 1915, pp. 1254-1255.

_____. "The Motion Picture Board of Trade," *Moving Picture World,* November 20, 1915, p. 1454.

_____. "War Films," *Moving Picture World,* September 19, 1914, p. 1617.

_____. "We Have Just Begun to Fight," *Moving Picture World,* March 27, 1915, p. 1902.

Carr, Henry C. "Capturing the Kaiser," *Photoplay,* IX (March, 1916), pp. 111-112.

Crain, Kenneth C. "Ohio Censors Watch All Films Closely," *Moving Picture World,* May 19, 1917, p. 1464.

_____. "Preparedness Film Stirs," *Moving Picture World,* December 18, 1915, p. 2219.

Cripps, Thomas R. "The Reaction of the Negro to *The Birth of a Nation,*" *The Historian,* XXV, No. 3 (May, 1963), pp. 344-362.

Dench, Ernest A. "Preserving the Great War for Posterity by the Movies," *Motion Picture Magazine,* July, 1915, pp. 89–91, p. 169.

Evans, Raymond. "USDA Motion Picture Service 1908–1943," *Business Screen,* V, No. 1 (1943), p. 20–32.

Flynn, William. "American Boys in France Filmed," *Moving Picture World,* September 9, 1916, p. 172.

Gladdish, William. "Sunday Shows in Toronto," *Moving Picture World,* November 13, 1915, p. 1335.

Halberg, J. H. "Will Regulate Use of Electricity," *Moving Picture World,* September 14, 1918, pp. 1541–1542.

Hanford, Judson C. "European Armies in Action," *Moving Picture World,* August 22, 1914, p. 1079.

Harrison, Louis R. "The Rights of Man," *Moving Picture World,* October 30, 1915, p. 813.

Hawley, Douglas. "Asking Whether Lightless Nights Save Coal," *Moving Picture News,* January 19, 1918, p. 406.

Isenberg, Micheal T. "The Mirror of Democracy: Reflections of the War Films of World War I, 1917–1919," *Journal of Popular Culture,* IX, No. 4 (1976), pp. 878–885.

Jackson, W. H. "War Time Picture Activities," *Moving Picture World,* August 11, 1917, pp. 924–925.

_____. "War Time Pictures," *Moving Picture World,* August 24, 1917, p. 769.

Johnson, Julian. "The Eagle's Wings," *Photoplay,* XI, No. 3 (February, 1917), p. 79.

_____. "The Shadow Stage," *Photoplay,* X, No. 1 (August, 1916), p. 135.

Landon, G. Warren. "Motion Pictures—An Essential Industry," *Moving Picture World,* July 27, 1918, p. 559–560.

Larson, Cedric, and James R. Mock. "Lost Files of the Creel Committee of 1917–1919," *Public Opinion Quarterly,* V (January, 1939), pp. 5–28.

Linz, Clarence L. "Congress Passes Federal Tax Bill," *Moving Picture World,* September 23, 1916, p. 1949.

_____. "Picture Men Urge Substitute War Tax," *Moving Picture World,* May 26, 1917, p. 1267.

Lyons, Timothy J. "Hollywood and World War I, 1914–1918," *Journal of Popular Film,* I, No. 1 (Winter, 1972), pp. 15–30.

Mackaye, Milton. "The Birth of a Nation," *Scribner's Magazine,* CII, No. 5 (November, 1939), pp. 40–49.

McQuade, Jasper. "Chicago Newsletter," *Moving Picture World,* January 9, 1915, p. 203.

_____. "Chicago Newsletter," *Moving Picture World,* November 6, 1915, p. 1142.

Merritt, Russell. "Dixon, Griffith and the Southern Legend," *Cinema Journal,* XII, No. 1 (Fall, 1972), pp. 26–45.

Orteyga, F. G. "Random Shots About Export," *Moving Picture World,* March 10, 1917, p. 1515.

Peet, Creighton. "Hollywood at War, 1915–1918," *Esquire,* September, 1936, pp. 60–63, p. 109.

Ray, J. L. "Mayor's Order Stops All War Pictures," *Moving Picture World,* June 23, 1917, p. 1974.

Shellman, J. M. "Maryland Censors Recall Certain War Film," *Moving Picture World,* May 12, 1917, p. 992.

Shores, Robert J. "The European War in Grantwood, New Jersey," *Moving Picture Magazine,* January, 1915, pp. 68–78.

Spears, Jack. "World War I on the Screen," *Films in Review,* Pt. (April, 1968), pp. 274–365.

Spedon, Sam. "The War Tax on Motion Pictures," *Moving Picture World,* June 23, 1917, p. 1416.

Sutcliffe, J. B. "British Notes," *Moving Picture World,* June 12, 1915, p. 1781.

_____. "British Notes," *Moving Picture World,* October 7, 1916, p. 81.

Tippett, J. D. "All War Pictures Fake," *Moving Picture World,* October 3, 1914, p. 50.
Weitzel, Edward. "The Little American," *Moving Picture World,* July 21, 1917, p. 471.
York, Cal. "Must Have Their Movies," *Photoplay,* XII (July, 1917), p. 153.
_____. "Plays and Players," *Photoplay,* XI (May, 1917), p. 63.
_____. "Plays and Players," *Photoplay,* XII (September, 1917), p. 110.


*Unsigned articles*

"Activities of the War Committees of the Motion Picture Industry," *Moving Picture World,*
    September 22, 1917, p. 1822.
"Advance Notes," *Moving Picture World,* August 15, 1914, p. 873.
"Aeroplane Clash between Creel and Universal," *Moving Picture World,* July 6, 1918, pp. 41–42.
"Ambulance Corps in France Filmed," *New York Times,* July 6, 1916, p. 11.
"America Invaded Again in Films," *New York Times,* June 7, 1916, p. 11.
"America Preparing," *New York Times,* July 11, 1916, p. 9.
"American Ambulance Pictures at Strand," *Moving Picture World,* December 23, 1916, p. 1781.
"American Cinema Commission Preparing," *Moving Picture World,* November 10, 1917, p. 842.
"American Film Invasion of Brazil," *Moving Picture World,* December 30, 1916, p. 1936.
"America's Answer Stirs War Spirit," *New York Times,* July 30, 1918, p. 9.
"Army to Investigate Hearst Tank Film," *New York Times,* June 25, 1918, p. 24.
"Attack on Creel," *New York Times,* April 11, 1918, p. 4.
"Attacks Creel Committee," *New York Times,* April 2, 1918, p. 7.
"Balfour Arouses Big War Benefit," *New York Times,* May 13, 1917, p. 3.
"Ban Lifted on Ordeal," *Moving Picture World,* June 12, 1915, p. 1731.
"The Battle Cry of Peace," *New York Times,* August 7, 1915, p. 8.
"Battle of Somme in Film," *New York Times,* September 30, 1916, p. 11.
"Big Jump in Film Exports," *Moving Picture World,* November 20, 1915, p. 1518.
"Big Opening for Vitagraph Feature," *Moving Picture World,* September 25, 1915, p. 2158.
"Black Tuesdays Mean Good Mondays," *Moving Picture World,* February 9, 1918, p. 807.
"Boosting the Liberty Loan," *Moving Picture World,* June 2, 1917, p. 1419.
"Brady Denounces Motion Picture War Tax," *New York Times,* July 16, 1916, Sec. I, p.14.
"British Fleet in Movies," *New York Times,* October 19, 1915, p. 2.
"Calendar of Licensed Releases," *Moving Picture World,* August 8, 1914, p. 887.
"Call Truce in Fight over Suppressed Film," *New York Times,* June 25, 1918, p. 24.
"Congressmen Hear Film Tax Proposal," *Moving Picture News,* July 6, 1918, pp. 43–44.
"Congressmen Inquire about Picturemaking," *Moving Picture World,* July 13, 1918, p. 188.
"Court Lifts the Hyphen out of Citizenship," *New York Times,* May 27, 1915, p. 5.
"Creel Accepts Congress Control," *New York Times,* June 14, 1918, p. 8.
"Creel Cuts Back Work," *New York Times,* July 10, 1918, p. 9.
"Creel Declines to Appear," *New York Times,* June 28, 1918, p. 8.
"Creel Explains Films," *New York Times,* June 29, 1918, p. 6.
"Creel to Lose Draft Age Men," *New York Times,* June 27, 1918, p. 5.
"Donald C. Thompson—Home from the War," *Moving Picture World,* December 25, 1915, p.
    2375.
"Donald Thompson's Famous War Pictures," *Moving Picture World,* February 6, 1915, p. 812.
"Essanay Cuts out Depressing Stories," *Moving Picture World,* June 9, 1917, p. 1605.
"Exhibitors Protest Lightless Nights," *Moving Picture World,* January 6, 1918, p. 120.
"Explanations Clear War-Film Row," *Moving Picture World,* July 13, 1918, p. 201.
"Facts and Comments," *Moving Picture World,* January 2, 1915, p. 43.
"Fake War Movies," *Literary Digest,* November 13, 1915, p. 2375.

"Fake War Pictures Stir East Side," *New York Times,* September 6, 1914, p. 6.
"Film Division Names Director Advisors," *Moving Picture World,* July 20, 1918, p. 363.
"Film Folk Doing Their Bit," *Photoplay,* XII (September, 1917), p. 111.
"Film Interests Mobilized," *New York Times,* July 12, 1917, p. 2.
"Film Men Form Board of Trade," *New York Times,* August 6, 1915, p. 6.
"Film of Battle of Arras Here," *New York Times,* July 7, 1917, p. 9.
"Films of Allied Soldiers," *New York Times,* October 7, 1917, Sec. I, p. 7.
"Films to Teach Fuel Saving," *Moving Picture News,* March 2, 1918, p. 1260.
"For Uncle Sam's Navy," *Moving Picture World,* June 3, 1916, p. 1755.
"France to Picture War," *New York Times,* April 14, 1915, p. 12.
"French Fighters in Films," *New York Times,* May 30, 1915, Sec. II, p. 3.
"Funds for Creel Reduced by House," *New York Times,* June 18, 1918, p. 7.
"General Films War Pictures," *Moving Picture World,* December 23, 1916, p. 1781.
"German Propaganda Works on a Cash Basis," *New York Times,* August 16, 1915, p. 3.
"Germans on the Screen," *New York Times,* September 21, 1915, p. 11.
"Germany and Its Armies of Today," *Moving Picture World,* January 13, 1917, p. 181.
"Go over the Top with Pershing," *Moving Picture World,* July 20, 1918, p. 358.
"Government Gives Enthusiastic Approval," *Moving Picture World,* September 23, 1918, p. 1855.
"Great Liberty Bond Hold-Up," *Photoplay,* XIII (December, 1917), p. 58.
"Great Naval Pictures by Lubin," *Moving Picture World,* January 2, 1915, p. 47.
"Greetings on Film," *New York Times,* December 31, 1915, p. 6.
"Guarding Old Glory," *Moving Picture World,* June 15, 1915, p. 1785.
"How Britain Prepared," *Moving Picture World,* March 25, 1916, p. 2025.
"How Britain Prepared," *New York Times,* May 30, 1916, p. 3.
"Hughes and T. R. in Movies," *New York Times,* August 26, 1916, p. 4.
"If My Country Should Call," *Moving Picture World,* September 16, 1916, p. 1823.
"The Industry and Liberty Bonds," *Moving Picture World,* June 23, 1917, p. 1946.
"Industry Backing Liberty Loan," *Moving Picture World,* June 9, 1917, p. 1617.
"Industry Declared Essential," *Moving Picture World,* September 7, 1918, p. 1386.
"Insists on Creel Inquiry," *New York Times,* March 15, 1918, p. 12.
"Italy at War in Films," *New York Times,* June 13, 1916, p. 9.
"Latest American Company in Canada," *Moving Picture World,* December 18, 1915, p. 2228.
"Liberty Bond Sales," *New York Times,* June 6, 1917, p. 3.
"Liberty, New Preparedness Serial," *Moving Picture World,* July 22, 1916, p. 644.
"Malitz's Connection Legitimate," *Moving Picture World,* September 14, 1915, p. 1624.
"Managers Fight Three-Day Closing," *Moving Picture World,* January 26, 1918, p. 537.
"Marines in Haiti in Film," *New York Times,* April 26, 1916, p. 11.
"Marines under Fire in Haiti," *Moving Picture World,* May 13, 1916, p. 1179.
"Memorandum on Motion Picture Accounts," July 10, 1916, Price, Waterhouse and Company, New York, pp. 1-12.
"Most Important Event of the Year," *Wid's Year Book,* [Later called *Film Daily Yearbook*] (1918; rpt. New York: Arno Press, 1971), unpaginated.
"Mothers of France," *Moving Picture World,* March 10, 1917, p. 1447.
"Motor Car Movies, New Camp Feature," *New York Times,* August 20, 1917, p. 5.
"Movies for Preparedness," *New York Times,* March 16, 1917, p. 6.
"Movies Mobilized to Aid in War Work," *New York Times,* July 29, 1917, Sec. II, p. 8.
"Movies Will Boost Latest French Loan," *New York Times,* November 25, 1915, p. 2.
"Moving Pictures an Essential Industry," *New York Times,* August 26, 1918, p. 9.
"A Nation's Peril," *Moving Picture World,* June 15, 1912, p. 1013.

"A Nation's Peril," *Moving Picture World*, November 27, 1915, p. 1675.
"Neutrality at Shows," *Moving Picture World*, June 5, 1916, p. 1164.
"New York Shelled on Movie Screen," *New York Times*, August 7, 1915, p. 8.
"No Cameras Going to Front," *Moving Picture World*, September 12, 1914, p. 1487.
"No New Movies until Influenza Ends," *New York Times*, October 10, 1918, p. 4.
"Observations," *Moving Picture World*, September 25, 1915, p. 2193.
"On Belgian Battlefields," *Moving Picture World*, December 12, 1914, p. 1057.
"On Dangerous Ground," *Moving Picture World*, January 13, 1917, p. 239.
"On the Firing Line with the Germans," *Moving Picture World*, January 5, 1916, p. 481.
"The Ordeal," *Moving Picture World*, November 14, 1914, p. 934.
"Our American Boys in the European War," *Moving Picture World*, July 22, 1916, p. 648.
"Pathe Plans Big Campaign," *Moving Picture World*, December 9, 1916, p. 1479.
"Patriotic and Red Cross Films," *Moving Picture World*, June 16, 1917, p. 1605.
"Patriotism and Nature," *Moving Picture World*, March 13, 1917, p. 2702.
"Pershing's Bookings Largest Ever," *Moving Picture World*, September 21, 1918, p. 1703.
"Plan to Control Industry for War," *New York Times*, April 8, 1918, p. 4.
"Preparedness Plea as Movie Theme," *New York Times*, August 6, 1915, p. 6.
"President Tells of Humbugs at Large," *New York Times*, January 28, 1916, p. 2.
"Prepare, President Wilson Pleads," *New York Times*, January 26, 1916, p. 1.
"Race for World's Trophy on," *Moving Picture World*, July 27, 1918, p. 531.
"Roosevelt at Film of American Valor," *New York Times*, September 24, 1916, Sec. I, p. 4.
"Secretary Praises Guarding Old Glory," *Moving Picture World*, December 25, 1915, p. 2406.
"See Big Invasion on Film," *New York Times*, August 11, 1915, p. 6.
"Sell Soda Tickets as Theatre Tickets," *New York Times*, September 21, 1915, p. 11.
"Show Artillery in Battle,"*New York Times*, August 27, 1917, p. 7.
"Show Tanks in Action," *New York Times*, May 21, 1917, p. 7.
"Theatres Dazed, Rally Quickly," *Moving Picture News*, February 2, 1918, p. 680.
"Trade Notes," *Moving Picture World*, September 5, 1914, p. 1343.
"Truce in Universal-Creel Row," *Moving Picture News*, July 6, 1918, p. 62.
"Uncle Sam's Defenders," *Moving Picture World*, December 9, 1916, p. 1478.
"Unpreparedness Pictured," *New York Times*, February 16, 1916, p. 3.
"Vanderbilt Backs War Relief Film," *New York Times*, January 17, 1917, p. 11.
"Vitagraph Stages Great Battle," *Moving Picture World*, September 9, 1915, p. 1674.
"Vitagraph Sues Ford for $1,000,000," *Moving Picture World*, September 8, 1915, p. 1667.
"Wants Baker to Tell of Film Agreement," *New York Times*, June 26, 1918, p. 7.
"War Cameraman's Kit," *Moving Picture World*, December 15, 1917, p. 1673.
"War Film Stopped; Hearst Influence on Creel Blamed," *New York Times*, June 29, 1918, p. 1.
"War Pictures For America," *New York Times*, October 28, 1917, Sec. I, p. 17.
"War Scenes in Lubin Features," *Moving Picture World*, October 6, 1915, p. 1113.
"Warn Motion Picture Men," *New York Times*, August 26, 1914, p. 9.
"Whole Industry Declared Essential," *Moving Picture News*, September 7, 1918, p. 154.

# Index